THE HUNT
FOR THE
SILVER KILLER

Praise for *The Silver Killer*

'A truly astonishing murder mystery – this is proper journalism.'
Jeremy Clarkson

'A book set to become a classic of the true crime genre. This is a page-turning thriller I couldn't put down.'
Sophy Ridge, Sky News

'When the suburban dream becomes the suburban nightmare. Shocking and powerful in equal measure. Investigative journalism at its finest.'
Nazir Afzal, former chief prosecutor for the north-west, author of *The Prosecutor*

'This is a skilful telling of a gripping true story about the investigation and detection of murder. Readers will be captivated, as I was, by the determined quest of one remarkable woman – risking her reputation and career to try and prove the presence of a serial killer among us.'
David James Smith, author of *Sleep of Reason*, *Supper with the Crippens*, *Young Mandela*

'Astonishingly good, a true story that grips like the very best thriller – I defy anyone to put this down.'
Peter James

'A shocking and thoroughly engaging work more terrifying than any horror story. An *I'll Be Gone in The Dark* for the North West of England.'
Janice Hallett, author of *The Appeal*

THE HUNT FOR THE SILVER KILLER

DAVID COLLINS

**SIMON &
SCHUSTER**

London · New York · Sydney · Toronto · New Delhi

First published in Great Britain by Simon & Schuster UK Ltd, 2022

1 3 5 7 9 10 8 6 4 2

Simon & Schuster UK Ltd
1st Floor
222 Gray's Inn Road
London WC1X 8HB

www.simonandschuster.co.uk
www.simonandschuster.com.au
www.simonandschuster.co.in

Simon & Schuster Australia, Sydney
Simon & Schuster India, New Delhi

A CIP catalogue record for this book
is available from the British Library

Hardback ISBN: 978-1-3985-05346
eBook ISBN: 978-1-3985-0535-3

Typeset in Perpetua by M Rules

Printed and bound by CPI Group (UK) Ltd, Croydon, CR0 4YY

MIX
Paper from
responsible sources
FSC® C171272

CONTENTS

THE HUNT
FOR THE
SILVER KILLER

PROLOGUE

It was April 2020. The first national coronavirus lockdown had ground the UK to a halt as the government placed restrictions on our daily lives to curb the spread of the virus. People were instructed to stay at home and avoid their family and friends, pubs and restaurants closed their doors, classrooms were emptied, and only one member of each household was allowed to enter a supermarket. The news had become an endless flurry of statistics about the pandemic, and at times it felt like the only story being reported. The *Sunday Times*'s regional office in Manchester had closed. I found myself reporting on the pandemic from a shed at the bottom of my garden.

One afternoon, working in my shed, I received a phone call from a source who was in possession of a confidential report. The author of the report was Stephanie Davies, the senior coroner's officer for Cheshire Police, a high-flyer who had been given two commendations by the chief constable and held a string of qualifications in death investigations, crime scenes and forensic science. Davies headed a team of thirteen civilian staff investigating sudden and unexpected deaths on behalf of the Cheshire coroner. The 179-page document was a review of two murder-suicides which had taken place in Wilmslow, Cheshire, in 1996 and 1999. Both cases involved elderly couples with no history of domestic violence, health problems or financial worries at the time of their deaths. They lived in large houses in one of the wealthiest areas outside London, a town where footballers and soap stars rub shoulders with businessmen and bankers, and violent crime was a rarity.

I read the report in one sitting. The graphic violence of the crimes was disturbing. Photographs of married couples lying side by side in twisted, bloodied bedsheets. The women, in particular, had been the focus of excessive violence: bludgeoned and stabbed, their wounds far in excess of what was required to kill. In each case, the police had concluded the killer was the husband, who had subsequently taken his own life. That would have been the end of the matter. Except that the senior coroner's officer, doubting the original findings of murder-suicide, had revisited the cases and arrived at her own conclusion. She believed the murder-suicides were in fact murders committed by a single offender, a serial killer, who had been active in the north-west of England since the mid-'90s. The killer she was proposing was subtle. He was forensically aware. But he had made mistakes. He had left behind clues which Davies had pieced together with the help of several leading homicide and forensic investigators. The report was known colloquially inside Cheshire Police as the 'Davies Review'.

The Davies Review was handed to senior detectives within Cheshire Police's major incident team in September 2018. It was then further expanded and updated in June 2020. Davies had concluded that innocent men were wrongly implicated for the murder of their wives. She believed the police and coroner service in Cheshire had committed a serious injustice. But her search for the truth about the Wilmslow killings would exact a heavy toll, placing her career, her health and even her liberty at risk.

Serial killers are rare creatures, rare enough that their names live on in public consciousness long after their crimes. Peter Sutcliffe. Ian Brady. Fred West. They are the bogeymen. The reason we listen out for the creak on the stairs. I came across such an individual once before. His name was Levi Bellfield. He specialised in blitz attacks on young women, using a heavy blunt object to batter them about the head in a flurry of hatred. I interviewed him when I was a cub reporter. I remain the only journalist who has spoken to Bellfield. At the time he was a prime suspect for the murder of Milly Dowler, a schoolgirl who vanished from Walton-on-Thames in Surrey in March 2002. During the interview Bellfield admitted to driving a red Daewoo car caught on CCTV shortly after Milly went missing. The admission placed him at the scene of Milly's disappearance. Two years later he was convicted at the Old Bailey for Milly's murder. Maria Woodall, the lead detective on the case, would later say my interview with Bellfield brought the evidence against him to a 'whole new level'.

Bellfield was cunning, but not so cunning that he avoided capture. The Davies Review detailed the work of a different type of killer. For years, he had existed only on paper and in the canteen gossip of Macclesfield Police Station. His crimes were stored in a box marked 'Special Interest' and kept inside a locked cupboard. Nobody knew what to do with them. They were anomalies. Wrinkles in the system that could not be ironed out. The police can often struggle with the unusual or unnatural, and serial killers can be harder to catch because their behaviour is more difficult to understand. Their need to kill can appear irrational, random and impulsive. The police have been trying since the Victorian era to turn detective work from an art form into a science in order to catch such killers more quickly. But a part of detective work will always rely upon intuition and a sharp eye.

Stephanie Davies was not the only person who believed a serial killer was at work in Cheshire. Her predecessor, Christine Hurst, the coroner's officer who dealt with the Wilmslow killings at the time, was also convinced the murders were carried out by a single offender. As this book will document, she raised her concerns at the time with police officers on both cases. Her concerns went unheeded.

In August 2020, the *Sunday Times* published a series of articles based on the findings of the Davies Review. This book is a continuation of that work. For the first time, it tells the remarkable stories of Christine Hurst and Stephanie Davies, two civilian investigators for Cheshire Police who battled against all the odds in the macho world of policing to expose what they believed to be the truth. It is the story of the hunt for the *Silver Killer*.

I

The Ainsworths

That Saturday lunchtime in Gravel Lane in Wilmslow, Cheshire, was like any other. Cars trundled to the shops, children kicked balls in the nearby playing field, and just up the road the tall, kindly figure of Howard Ainsworth could be seen taking advantage of the spring weather to potter about his garden. His neighbour, Margaret Farror, who lived in the house adjoining his own, popped over for a catch-up. He saw her coming and straightened up from the flower beds of tulips and pansies to crack a joke, warning her to stay away.

'I wouldn't come too close,' he said. 'Bea's got the lurgy. You'll end up catching it yourself if you're not careful.'

'Oh? Poor Bea. What's wrong with her?'

'Some sort of stomach bug. She's been vomiting all night. I had to help her to the bathroom a few times.'

Howard was being his usual friendly self. He was tall and physically strong for a man of seventy-nine. He had a kindly face, a side-sweep of receding silver hair and a slightly ruddy complexion. Spectacles perched on top of a bulbous nose. His typical attire was a short-sleeved shirt and trousers. He was relaxed with people he knew, but with those he didn't his manner could come across as a little brusque, typical for an ex-army man of his generation.

He had spent the Second World War fighting the Japanese in Burma. He watched his friends die there. He would never forget it. He left the army and spent most of his life working for the local council maintaining parks. It was steady work, enough to afford a semi-detached house on Gravel Lane, a property which had soared in value. Not that he would ever move. He lived with his wife, Florence, known as Bea to her family and friends. Her middle name was Beatrice, and she much preferred it. They were proud of their home and kept it immaculately tidy. They were fastidious when it came to household chores and liked everything to be just so. This was the house where they had raised their only child, John, before he grew up and moved away. John lived in Derby now, but still visited with the grandchildren.

It was fair to say the Ainsworths were a well-known couple in the town of Wilmslow, largely because of Bea's old job at the funeral directors, which had an office just around the corner. She would often be stopped in the street by the bereaved families she had helped over the years. Howard and Bea were still physically active. Howard would be seen cycling around Wilmslow on a bicycle with a basket at the front. They both enjoyed walking, and would drive up to the Lake District to get lost in its hills. Howard felt most at peace in the countryside, rather than the busy urban centres, which is why he enjoyed living in Wilmslow so much, a small town that still very much felt like a village, particularly where he lived.

At 2 p.m. Margaret saw Howard mowing his front lawn. Nothing unusual about that. She approached him to get an update on Bea's condition. Howard said she seemed to be improving and had managed a small amount to eat and drink.

'That's good news,' Margaret said. 'Well, if there's anything I can do, you know where I am.'

That was the last time Margaret saw him. She didn't see Bea at all that weekend. She had spoken to her on Monday. Bea had appeared her normal self. There was nothing to suggest anything untoward. Bea was considerably smaller in size than her husband. Howard was large and lumbering, whereas Bea was petite and bird-like, with a thin waist and delicate wrists. Like many women of her age, she kept her white curly hair short and cropped above the neck. She was known among friends as being 'easy company'. Easier than her husband, perhaps. Howard could be more reserved. His work as a gardener for Manchester Corporation, later renamed Manchester City Council, had led him in his retirement to maintain an almost professional interest in his own garden, keeping the lawn, hedges and flower beds in perfect condition. He would leave seeds out for the wild birds. Neighbours often joked their garden was like a wild bird sanctuary. He was good with his hands and an excellent car mechanic, teaching his son the basics of vehicle maintenance in his typical no-nonsense way.

Howard's rather blunt manner had led to a minor squabble with their neighbours, Halton and Jacqueline Cummings. The Cummings family had had an extension built onto the side of their home and there was a dispute over the boundary wall. Halton never spoke to Howard again after that. It wasn't a major dispute; just an unfortunate disagreement which had cooled relations. Jacqueline maintained a cordial relationship with Howard and Bea, and exchanged polite greetings over the fence, or when passing them in the street.

In the last few days, Howard had been worried about Bea's

illness and had contacted the Kenmore Medical Centre to report that she was vomiting repeatedly. An appointment was booked for Dr Claire Redhead to carry out a non-urgent house call on Friday at 10 a.m. Before her visit Dr Redhead checked Bea's medical notes on the computer, which showed no past medical history of note and no prescriptions for any form of medication.

A couple of months earlier, Bea had undergone her '75+ Health Examination', a standard health check carried out by the clinic. The practice nurse had recorded a normal examination: nothing out of the ordinary about her physical or mental condition. In fact, it had been two years since Bea had last visited a doctor, when she was suffering from a sore throat. For exercise she would regularly walk five to seven miles a day and swim between ten and twelve lengths non-stop in the swimming pool. Her GP considered her a fit and healthy woman.

Howard stayed at his wife's side during the examination on Friday. He was nursing Bea in the master bedroom at the rear of the house, where the windows looked out onto their back garden. Bea's main complaint was vomiting. She had been retching since Thursday. The vomiting would start twenty minutes or so after eating or drinking, leaving her feverish and dizzy. Despite the rather alarming symptoms, which were causing Bea some distress, Dr Redhead found nothing to suggest it was a serious infection. Bea had no sensations of vertigo, tinnitus or deafness. No headaches, rashes or coughing. Dr Redhead decided Bea was suffering from a bout of gastroenteritis, a common form of tummy bug caused by infection and inflammation of the digestive system. Although unpleasant, Bea's symptoms would only last for another twenty-four to forty-eight hours. After that she could expect to feel a great deal better.

Bea was given an intramuscular injection of 12.5mg of Stemetil, a drug used to treat nausea, vomiting and dizziness, and instructed to drink plenty of fluids. Dr Redhead told them to call the medical centre again if she developed any new symptoms, but she reassured them there was nothing serious or long-lasting about the bug. Bea was a fit and healthy 78-year-old, and Dr Redhead expected her to shrug off an ailment like this in a matter of days.

Like Bea, Howard was in good shape. Dr Redhead was not his regular GP, but his medical file recorded that he had no serious ailments, either. Howard had also recently visited the medical centre for his '75+ Health Examination', where the nurse recorded full fitness and a 'normal state of mind'. Dr Redhead left their house confident that Bea would make a full recovery and happy with the care Howard was providing. She was the last known person to see Bea alive.

The Ainsworths had been retired since the late '70s. Howard had left the council, while Bea had quit her secretarial job at Albert R. Slack, the funeral director's. 'Slack's the name, stiff's the game,' their son John and his wife used to joke. In 1978, Bea had told her boss, Robin Currie the funeral director, that she wanted to retire and spend more time with her husband. She was a big loss to Currie. Bea was popular with the customers: Currie would describe her as 'pleasant', 'easy-going', 'reliable' and 'competent'. During weekdays, she would work in the front office from 9 a.m. to 3 p.m., then take a short walk home around the playing fields. Sometimes Howard would meet her. They disliked being apart.

The last time they had been separated for any significant period of time was during the war. While he was fighting in

Burma, Howard didn't see Bea for six years. They remained engaged, and got married on his return. But the Howard who came back from overseas wasn't the same happy-go-lucky lad who had gone off in his twenties to fight for his country. He saw many friends die in combat. He rarely spoke of it. Not to Bea or to his son John, who with his wife Rosemarie gave him two grandchildren, Peter and Heather. Rosemarie considered John's parents a little 'stiff and starched' for her taste. John and Rosemarie had recently been through a divorce, which had been tough on the family.

Their neighbour Margaret slept soundly that Saturday night. Her bedroom was separated from the Ainsworths' bedroom by a brick wall. She woke the next morning oblivious to what had occurred overnight inside the house next door. There had been no screams that she could tell of. No cries for help through the walls. Just the usual – silence. Margaret got herself ready and at 11.30 a.m. went out into her front garden to water the plants. The Ainsworths' curtains were still closed. Strange, she thought. They were always up by now. In twenty-four years of living next door to the Ainsworths, Margaret had never known them to sleep in so late. She knocked on the front door and tapped on the windows. No response. She was starting to get worried.

She knocked on Jacqueline Cummings's door and told her about the curtains still being closed. Margaret wondered if she should go inside the house to check up on them. No, said Jacqueline: it would be better to call the police – Howard might not take kindly to them poking around inside the house. There was also the possibility that if anything had happened to them, an intruder might still be inside the property. Margaret agreed. Something just didn't feel right. Her heart thumping, she returned to her house and took the nerve-wracking decision to pick up the phone and call 999.

'Hello, police? I would like to report something strange about next door . . .'

At 11.45 a.m. on Sunday, 28 April 1996, a message crackled on the walkie-talkie belonging to WPC Jennifer Eastman, collar number 2913. It was a request to check out No. 85 Gravel Lane. She was on standard patrol duties in Wilmslow at the time, and thought it would be a quick call to check up on an elderly couple – fifteen minutes, tops. The 25-year-old was new to the job, at the beginning of what turned out to be a lifelong career in the police. She drove her marked police car into the town centre and picked up PC Neal Miller, who was also out on patrol. Miller was two years her junior.

They parked outside the house in Gravel Lane to find the Ainsworths' curtains still drawn. Margaret was waiting for them. She was the person who had called the police, she explained. She hadn't seen Howard or Bea all morning, and Howard would usually be out in his garden by now. Bea hadn't been well the last few days, she went on – something to do with a virus that was making her vomit – and Howard had been helping her to the toilet. The Ainsworths were creatures of routine: early risers. They weren't on holiday either: as far as she knew, the car was still in the garage. It didn't make any sense.

Eastman walked to the back of the house and found the rear kitchen door unlocked. The officers pushed the door open and walked inside the clean but slightly musty-smelling interior, Eastman and Miller first, followed by Margaret. They walked through the kitchen, searching the downstairs living room, the front room, the utility room and downstairs bathroom. No sign of Howard or Bea. No sign of a disturbance or a struggle, either. Leaving Margaret in the hallway, Eastman and Miller went up the gloomy stairs. At the top of the stairs on a sideboard, was a yellow piece of paper. Something was written on it in capital letters. Three words. **DO NOT RUSUCACATE** [resuscitate].

Eastman and Miller glanced at one another and headed towards the main bedroom. The door was open to the upstairs landing and they could see a pair of feet dangling off the bed, framed against the flowery yellow wallpaper. Inside, lying in the double bed, were Howard and Bea, side by side in blood-soaked sheets. Dead. Not just dead: Bea had been butchered. She was on the right-hand side, closest to the door, her face turned a little towards Howard. Most of her head was soaked in blood. Against her cheek was a pillow patterned in white, yellow and blue rectangles. Most of the pillow was crimson.

But that wasn't the most shocking part. Not by a long shot.

Somebody had stabbed a kitchen knife into Bea's head. All that could be seen of the knife was a black handle protruding from the centre of her forehead. Blood had seeped down her face to her right arm and collected in a red pool between the bodies, staining the mint-green bedsheets. Her crumpled white nightie had been yanked up at the hip to expose her pubic area. She had red scuff marks on her knees and her left hand lingered uselessly around her midriff, her other hand tucked awkwardly underneath her chin. On her ring finger was a gold wedding ring, and on her left wrist a gold watch. If this was a burglary gone wrong, the burglar had left some valuable items behind.

Howard was beside Bea in the bed. His head was covered by a clear polythene bag which was spattered in fine droplets of blood. The bag sat on his head, cone-shaped, like a ceremonial hood from some forbidden religion. His right leg was crossed over his left. His left arm was trapped awkwardly under his body. His right arm was laid across his chest. His head and neck were propped up against the headboard, again in a rather awkward resting position. His pale-blue pyjamas were remarkably clean. He had a few spots of blood on his top, but nothing compared to Bea, whose entire head, shoulder and side of her body facing Howard were drenched in blood. His pyjama bottoms were stained with urine.

On Howard's side of the bed was a table with a portable TV set. The TV was switched off. In front of the TV was a bedside clock, empty tumbler glasses and a bottle containing twenty-two brown-and-grey pills. On the carpet next to the bed on Howard's side was a ligature. On Bea's side of the bed was a bedside table decorated by pink and white flowers in an ornate brown vase. Next to the vase was a hammer with a long wooden handle and a well-worn hammerhead. Also on the table was a shoe heel, a shoe brush, a picture frame and a white bowl.

PC Eastman walked slowly from the bedroom and stopped a moment to steel herself. This was a sight that would stay with her forever. She went down the stairs to where Margaret was waiting anxiously in the downstairs hallway and gently escorted Margaret out of the house, leaving Miller to secure the bedroom as a crime scene, ensuring that nothing was touched until the detectives, forensics experts and scenes of crime officers (SOCOs) had arrived. Eastman used her radio to speak to the control room. Two bodies found. Elderly couple. Female with knife in head. Male with bag over his head. No sign of forced entry. *Request immediate assistance.*

2

The Gucci Gang

The CID offices on the upper floor of Wilmslow's Hawthorn Street police station were quiet apart from the occasional shuffle of paperwork and the low hum of the police radio. The detectives would keep the radio switched on in the background in case they picked up on anything which required urgent assistance. Working the Sunday shift were Detective Inspector Brian Hibbitt, Detective Sergeant Richard Woolley and Detective Constable Chris Warren. Their office was open-plan with a view looking out over trees and parkland in the direction of the fire station.

Hibbitt had his own office, separate from the banks of desks. Dark-haired and thick-set, he was a good old-fashioned DI who wasn't averse to listening to new ideas from his younger detectives. His team at Wilmslow consisted of four detective sergeants and twelve detective constables. A superintendent was in overall charge of the police station, responsible for the oversight of around ninety staff, including uniformed officers, CID and the custody suite team.

Hibbitt got on well with DS Woolley, a tall man with dark hair and a passing resemblance to Robert Mitchum, one of the 'golden oldie' stars of Hollywood, although nobody would ever tell him in case it gave him a big head. Woolley was straight-forward, dogmatic and great company down the pub. Twenty years in the force had given him a reputation as a formidable investigator. He once uncovered a drugs gang in possession of 400 kilos of cannabis. One of the major players had escaped to Spain, known as the Costa del Crime due to the number of fugitive criminals living there. Woolley waited eight years before nabbing him in Madrid.

Wilmslow CID were a tight-knit crew, one big family who lived and breathed policing. The detectives got the job done and didn't mind a pint or two down the Boddington Arms after work. Back in the nineties, being an officer in Cheshire Police was like being a soldier in the army. There were strict chains of command. People did what they were told. Officers still stood up in meetings when the superintendent walked into the room. But that was put to one side down the pub, where people drank hard and smoked heavy. Nevertheless, the detectives at neigh-bouring Macclesfield Police Station thought Wilmslow CID a bit stuck-up. Maybe it was because they worked in well-to-do Wilmslow. Or maybe it was because the detectives would wear smart suits from Slaters in Manchester. Their sharp dressing earned Wilmslow CID a nickname from their counterparts at Macclesfield, the divisional headquarters. They called them the 'Gucci gang'. The nickname stuck. *Eh up, here come the Gucci gang. Criminals beware!*

Every copper in Cheshire Police was envious of the facilities available to those lucky enough to be based at Hawthorn Street 'nick'. Its custody suite meant suspects could be arrested, questioned in one of the interview rooms and locked up in a cell, all within the police station: no messing around having to transport suspects around Cheshire to other locations. The only downside to the building was the wasps, which would spring out from nests to harass the thin blue line of Wilmslow every single summer, driving the detectives mad as they chased the latest intruder around the office with a rolled-up newspaper and some insect spray.

Hibbitt and Woolley got the call. Two bodies found in a house in Gravel Lane, just a few streets from the station. Could they provide assistance to the uniformed officers at the scene? They arrived at the Ainsworths' house to find Eastman and Miller guarding the property. Woolley and Hibbitt went upstairs to carry out some initial observations of the scene. The first and most obvious clue was the **DO NOT RUSUCACATE** note at the top of the stairs. Woolley, acting as the exhibits officer, meaning he was in charge of gathering up and cataloguing the evidence found in the house, logged the item as RGW/5.

Woolley entered the Ainsworths' bedroom to inspect Howard's and Bea's bodies. He had rarely witnessed such violence in his two decades with the constabulary. Cheshire's police surgeon, Dr Leo Caprio – dark hair, glasses and a distinctly Italian look – arrived to certify the deaths in line with standard procedure and give his first impressions of the medical cause of death. Woolley identified a number of important clues in the bedroom. On the dressing table adjacent to the bed was a piece of yellow writing paper. The paper contained the name, address and telephone number for Howard and Bea's son, John Ainsworth. This piece of evidence was logged by Woolley as RGW/1. Beside the writing paper was a separate pad containing two pages of handwritten notes. At the bottom of the letter was Howard's signature. The letter read the following:

3.30 a.m. Sunday

Coroner

Bea when sick on Thursday evening and vomited continuously till I rang Kenmore (Medical Centre) at 8.30 — sent a Dr by 10.05 who checked Bea and said she had caught a virus which accounted for her falling over or loss of balance. Her sickness went but gradually she could not stomach and I had to carry her to the lavatory.

She had difficult in moving in bed — stares fixed in the distance and has become delirious. It looks as tho our lives have gone so have given her some sleeping tablets and I will have to throttle her as she would [not] be able to use the bag method. That is the method I have to use.

We have had a good life together — at the funeral we don't want persons — flowers or mourners at the cremation.

Howard Ainsworth

As far as suicide letters go, the note was an unusual one for a number of reasons. The final thoughts of a person just before they die are usually addressed to a loved one, rather than Her Majesty's Coroner. Much of the letter dealt with the logistics of the doctor's visit as well as Bea's symptoms. Again, this was highly unusual. Suicide notes are typically emotive, focusing on extreme positive or negative emotions. They might detail the reason for the decision. Sometimes they will articulate regrets about the impact of the suicide on loved ones left to deal with the consequences.

Then there was the line from Howard that their 'lives have gone', despite evidence that Bea's tummy bug was minor. Just thirteen hours before the note had been written, Margaret had said, Howard was optimistic about his wife's recovery – 'cheery', 'happy', even 'cracking jokes' were the words she used. A few hours later, Howard had apparently changed his mind and decided the world was coming to an end.

The detectives also noted that the plan proposed in Howard's letter had not been carried out. Howard said he would give Bea sleeping tablets and throttle her, but the toxicology would later reveal no sleeping pills in Bea's system: just a small amount of alcohol. Instead of pills and strangulation, Bea's head had been smashed repeatedly with a hammer, followed by a six-inch stainless-steel knife being driven into her head so deeply it punctured her left optic nerve and entered the cerebellum. The effort required to puncture her skull with the blade and push it into the mid-brain would have been considerable. The investigators wondered if the hammer might have been used to bash the butt of the knife while it was placed against her forehead, like hammering a nail into a piece of wood.

Two hammers were found in the upstairs rooms. One hammer was discovered in the bedroom on the bedside table next to the suicide note. This was a 'ball-pein hammer' and had two heads, one flat and the other, known as the pein, more rounded. The rounded end can be used for working metal, known as peining.

The second hammer was found in the upstairs bathroom, lying horizontally across the plughole in an old-fashioned sink with silver taps marked COLD and HOT. Around the sink was a brick of orange soap and a shaving brush, the sort you might find in a Turkish barber's shop. This hammer looked older than the one in the bedroom. The head had a blunt end with a pointed back and had traces of blood on it. There was blood in the plughole. The hammer had been washed down in the sink. Detectives believed this was the hammer used to belabour Bea's head, while the hammer in the bedroom may have been used to knock the butt of the knife so the sharp end penetrated through her skull. Woolley would ask the forensic scientists from the Home Office's forensic science laboratory to check out this theory.

The suicide note in the bedroom was strong evidence to suggest that Howard had murdered his wife and then killed himself, even if the murder didn't quite follow the method he described. But something else was puzzling some of the officers and staff who attended the crime scene. If Howard was about to take his own life, why wash down the murder weapon in the sink? It seemed unlikely to be out of cleanliness. By that point the bedroom and the bedsheets would have been bathed in blood. Washing a murder weapon was more common when an offender was trying to get away with their crime and evade the attentions of the police investigation.

The hammers and the knife in Bea's forehead were sent to the lab for forensic analysis. Blood samples were taken from Howard and Bea to determine their blood grouping, and swabs of blood were taken from Howard's hands to see if Bea's blood was on them. The options open to the detectives were rather limited. This was 1996. Back then, there was no such thing as trace DNA testing. In terms of forensics, Woolley had to operate using the simple assumption, 'If you can't see it, you can't test it.' Aside from fingerprint tests, only evidence visible to the eye, such as blood, could be sent to the lab for analysis.

Other clues were found in the main bedroom. A second note was discovered on the table next to the bedroom window. It looked as though Howard had scribbled down some of Bea's tummy bug symptoms, like crib notes, perhaps for the doctor's visit two days earlier, or perhaps for the call to the Kenmore receptionist. The note said that Bea was 'fit 78' and 'walks 5–7 miles in the hills'. It then said she 'sleeps constantly, makes little conversation'.

Beside the note was a glass bottle containing 22 chlormethiazole tablets. Six tablets were missing from the bottle. The dose was labelled as 'one or two capsules at night' and contained the warning: *Avoid alcoholic drink. Causes drowsiness which may persist until the next day, if affected do not drive or operate machinery.* Neither Howard nor Bea had a prescription for chlormethiazole on their medical records. How they had managed to obtain the bottle of pills remains a mystery.

Woolley had the tablets tested at Chorley Laboratory by a forensic scientist called Michael Hammond. Hammond was asked to establish what type of drug was in the tablets, how long traces could be expected to remain in the body and for what purpose they might be prescribed. After a few weeks he reported back that the drugs had a sedative, tranquillising and anticonvulsant activity. They were likely to cause drowsiness and sedation due to their depressant effect on the central nervous system. Chlormethiazole was a drug used to control the symptoms arising from acute alcohol withdrawal and was sometimes prescribed to treat restlessness and agitation, particularly in the elderly. It could also be used to treat insomnia in older people. Hammond said the drug may not be detectable in the blood in the morning after a single night-time dose, although it could be detected for far longer periods of time in the urine.

The police had both Howard's and Bea's bloods and urine tested by a clinical biochemist based at East Cheshire NHS Trust. The results came back negative for drugs. No pills were taken, despite the bottle being at arm's length. The findings posed another difficult question for the inquiry team. Why would Howard not take the tablets before putting the bag over his head, as he said he would in his note? Why would he make his suicide more difficult?

Woolley searched every room with the help of another detective and a SOCO. SOCOs, now called CSIs by modern police forces, were not police officers but support staff who gathered forensic evidence at crime scenes to help with the detection of crime. The SOCO took a number of colour photographs of the Ainsworths' bedroom with the bodies in the bed from different angles as well as pictures of the other significant finds around the house, such as the suicide note, the washed hammer in the bathroom sink and the note found at the top of the stairs. In what was a first for Wilmslow CID, they also filmed the scene, and would later watch the footage back when they decamped to the office.

Woolley was searching the sitting room when he came across some paperwork in the top drawer of a cabinet. The paperwork belonged to the Voluntary Euthanasia Society. There was a leaflet called *How to Die with Dignity*. On the floor next to the cabinet was another leaflet called *Bequeathing for a Better World*. In the same room, a piece of paper torn from a notepad had details about a suicide method. It provided information about how many tablets to consume.

The note said the back door should be left unlocked, a note of goodbye left behind, and a message warning not to resuscitate in the event of being discovered. Again, the word resuscitate was spelled incorrectly. The final step was to take a bag and place it over the head, which would give 'no pain' or 'discomfort', according to the note. It was Howard's euthanasia plan. Tablets to cause drowsiness and numb the pain, and then the bag over the head. A standard method for euthanasia supporters, which he had not followed.

The evidence found in the house was catalogued and handed over to the exhibits manager at Wilmslow Police Station. The clues were starting to come together. A narrative was beginning to form. There was the suicide note. A belief in euthanasia. A hammer and knife used on Bea, but a plastic bag for Howard. Detectives believed it was a case of murder-suicide. For reasons unknown to the investigation team, Howard had gone beserk, killed his wife and then himself.

At 4 p.m. on Sunday, Howard's and Bea's bodies were removed by Robin Currie, the undertaker for Bea's old firm, Albert R. Slack. Currie was on the police rota to deal with any sudden and unexpected deaths in the Wilmslow area. He was able to formally identify Howard and Bea to the police, saving their son, John, the grim task of attending the mortuary and viewing the bodies. PC Christopher Warren followed Currie to Macclesfield District General Hospital and oversaw the bodies as they were booked into the mortuary in preparation for the post-mortem examination.

Currie was shocked, like many others in the community. Howard and Bea were well-known in Wilmslow. Nobody had seen it coming. The grocery stores, hairdressers and coffee shops were full of chatter about their killings. Heard about Howard and Bea? But they were such a lovely couple. Ah, yes, but just goes to show, nobody knows what happens behind closed doors. Gossip spread that Bea had terminal cancer, and Howard, a known supporter of euthanasia, had decided to end her life and his own before it got too late. The rumour had no basis in fact.

The day after their bodies were found, their son, John, was ushered into his parents' house by two detectives. At the age of forty-four, John was entering something of a rough patch in his life after his recent divorce from his wife Rosemarie. He drove up from Derby after a police officer knocked on his door in the early hours of Monday morning to inform him that both his parents were dead. Accompanied by a trusted friend, John checked the house over, but found nothing unusual. There was nothing missing. Nothing had been stolen, so far as he could tell. He walked into his parents' bedroom to find it immaculate. The walls, carpet and bed had been scrubbed clean. There wasn't a drop of blood to be found. The SOCOs had been instructed to remove all trace of the killings before John's arrival.

After the visit to Gravel Lane, John was escorted to Wilmslow Police Station. He was shown the piece of paper found in his parents' bedroom with his name and address in Derby. He confirmed that it was his father's handwriting. He was not shown the suicide note. It was considered too distressing. John said the last time he had seen his mother and father was two weeks ago. He had visited them at home for a couple of hours – arriving at 5.30 p.m. and leaving around 7.30 p.m. There was no special reason for the visit. He tried to see his parents once a month.

He was aware of his parents' belief in euthanasia. Howard had spoken several times about his suicide pact with his mother: once their health went, Howard had told his son, they would end their lives with dignity, rather than become a burden. They firmly believed the decision should be their choice. It was their right to decide when to die and nobody else's. John told the police that when his father discussed the suicide pact, his mother had always been present in the room. They were in it together. Despite this, John had always harboured a suspicion that his father's conviction was stronger than his mother's. His mother was likely to go along with whatever his father said.

The witness statement from John, combined with the suicide note and the belief in euthanasia, made it an open and shut case for the police. Howard had murdered Bea, apparently because her tummy bug made their lives unliveable. It didn't make much sense. But then, they were elderly. Perhaps it didn't have to. It could be explained by a moment of madness from Howard. A random act of cruelty. A husband who had snapped and wreaked terrible violence upon his wife. Such acts of domestic violence were uncommon, but far from unknown. Perhaps at the last minute Bea had refused to go through with their long-prepared euthanasia pact. Maybe Howard had viewed her decision as a betrayal of their agreement and decided to take the matter into his own hands.

This was the official line of the police inquiry. But not everyone was convinced by this version of events. There were those within Cheshire Police who harboured serious doubts about Howard being the killer. Police investigations can be like jigsaw puzzles. They are often pieced together to provide the most likely possible outcome. But what if that conclusion contained contradictory evidence? What would happen if an alternative hypothesis were offered to explain the same crime – one which conflicted with the narrative being offered by the police inquiry team? One investigator was about to find out. And it would start with two packages of evidence addressed to the coroner's officer for the district of Macclesfield in Cheshire.

3

Growing Doubts

It was late April in 1996, and Christine Hurst, Coroner's Officer for Cheshire Police, had just returned from two weeks in Portugal where she had been visiting family with her husband. Boasting a nice even tan, Hurst walked into her office in Macclesfield Police Station at 9 a.m. to catch up on her post and look through the Form 92s which had arrived overnight, otherwise known as 'sudden-death forms'. The forms were sent in by police officers who had attended a non-suspicious sudden death in the community. It could be anything: a heart attack victim, someone who had fallen down the stairs, or a person who had committed suicide.

Two big brown envelopes sat in her in-tray. She opened them up. It was the Ainsworths' case in Wilmslow. She looked through the crime scene photographs. She had never seen such violence before. The bedroom was covered in blood. At first glance, it looked like the work of a psychopath. The police were saying the husband was the killer. Hurst wasn't so sure.

Hurst, aged forty-three at the time, with short flaxen hair, glasses, rounded cheeks and a warm smile, had been a coroner's officer at Cheshire Police for the last three years. It had not been an easy experience, especially when she arrived. Her predecessors in the role had all been retired police officers. She was a civilian. And a woman. Life was made difficult for her at first. But she was tough. She was resilient. She didn't quit and she worked hard to prove herself.

Hurst had a background in nursing, rather than policing. She had trained at the old Liverpool Royal Infirmary and worked as a general nurse on and off for twelve years, having two sons during that time. Coming from a nursing background had its advantages: much of the work of a coroner's officer can be about gathering medical material relating to the person who has died. Hurst would eventually devise the first ever nationwide medical course for coroner's officers.

Hurst was raised in Liverpool as the eldest of eight children and got a job when she left school at sixteen. Women of her generation from the North-West often went into four lines of work: nursing, secretarial, teaching or shopkeeping. Hurst had quit nursing and worked for a while as a secretary, but desk work for a private company was not for her: she missed the public service aspect of nursing. Some people are motivated by money; Hurst was motivated by the desire to help people, particularly those who were suffering bereavement. She had lost loved ones and knew what it felt like: one of her sisters, who had diabetes, had died aged twenty-nine. She had lost her mother two years before that.

When she saw a job advertised in the local paper for a coroner's officer in Macclesfield, she wasn't entirely sure what the role would entail. Her husband, Pete, a divorce lawyer, was able to provide a basic outline. Coroner's officers will investigate a death on behalf of the coroner, obtain all the information necessary and make a report so the coroner can decide whether to proceed with a post-mortem examination or an inquest. Hurst was intrigued. The job meant helping families find out the truth about the death of their loved ones. She would be employed by Cheshire Police but working under the direction of the senior coroner for Cheshire at the time, John Hibbert.

In 1993, Hurst applied for the job and got it, becoming one of the first civilian coroner's officers in the country, and was based at Macclesfield Police Station, the divisional headquarters. Her appointment was a culture shock to the police officers at the station. Back then the uniformed officers and detectives were almost entirely men, and in some quarters there was strong disapproval that Hurst had got the job over a police officer. The role had always been carried out by an ex-copper, and there were doubts as to whether she would be capable of the investigative work required. Macclesfield Police Station in the early '90s was a rather macho and misogynistic world, where groups of men would pop in to the Macclesfield canteen from stations miles away to avail themselves of the station's famous cooked breakfast – the best around, with the exception, perhaps, of the breakfast at Longsight Police Station canteen and its Spam fritters – but that was in a different force area altogether.

Hurst would never forget her first day in the office. On the wall opposite her desk somebody had pinned up a letter, right in her line of sight. The letter had been written by the local GP group she would have to deal with most days to conduct her sudden-death inquiries. 'We do not agree with the role of the Macclesfield coroner's officer being civilianised,' the letter read. 'Any mistakes in casework will result in an immediate written complaint to the office of the Chief Constable for Cheshire Constabulary.'

In many ways Christine Hurst was a gentle soul. But there was a toughness to her. Push her and she would push back, harder. Working in the world of policing wasn't always easy: she experienced both bullying and sexual harassment. But she beat the bullies and the sex pests to build a successful career in the police force which spanned twenty-three years. By the time she finished she had personally investigated 12,000 sudden deaths, later leading a team that during her time in charge in the county of Cheshire would investigate a total of more than 75,000 deaths.

She would provide evidence to the government's Harold Shipman inquiry relating to how coroner's officers should operate, and would repeatedly alert police and hospitals to suspicious cases, some of which went on to become major criminal inquiries. She became a founding member of the Coroner's Officers and Staff Association, where she held, at different times, the position of treasurer, deputy chair and chair, helping the Home Office, the Department of Constitutional Affairs, the Ministry of Justice and the Department of Health devise policy and procedure around the UK's coronial system. Her career brought with it a deep sense of satisfaction that in some small way she had helped families in their time of greatest need.

By 1996, Hurst was dealing with around 800 sudden death cases each year, of which roughly eighty would result in a full public inquest. Her job meant speaking to police officers and GPs, gathering information about the circumstances of the death, and any medical information about the person, in order to inform the pathologist and the coroner of any medical history that might have contributed to the person's death.

If someone was found dead at home, the first question Hurst

would ask is why they had died. What happened? She would speak to the family and the closest relatives to uncover any helpful information about past illnesses, mental health problems, social and medical history. She would build that into a report for the coroner along with any evidence from hospital doctors and GPs. The coroner could then decide whether or not to have a post-mortem examination, or whether a doctor should issue a medical certificate as to cause of death without a post-mortem, and then finally if an inquest should be held.

The fatality could be a road-traffic collision. A person who had walked in front of a train. Somebody found hanged in the woods. An old person who had died in a care home. Hurst never knew what would come across her desk next. She got on well with the chief coroner for Cheshire, John Hibbert, an old hand, avuncular and trustworthy, and the sort of coroner who didn't like putting families through the rigours of the process too much. His inquests, therefore, had a tendency to be quite short and to the point.

Inside the big brown envelopes on her desk that morning Hurst found two booklets containing crime scene and mortuary photographs for the Ainsworths' case, sent by the SOCOs, who were based in an office just down the corridor. She had been assigned coroner's officer for the case of Howard and Bea Ainsworth. Their deaths had been in the news. TRAGIC MYSTERY OF A DEVOTED COUPLE, said one headline in the *Manchester Evening News*. Neighbours had 'wept', the article said, at the deaths of the 'devoted nature-loving couple'. The newspaper said the police had found 'notes in the house' and believed 'no one else was involved in the deaths'.

She took the glossy colour photos from the booklets and

spread them out on her desk. The first photograph she picked up was of Howard, lying on the trolley in the mortuary at Macclesfield General Hospital, his head covered by a plastic bag. But it wasn't the bag which snagged her attention; she had seen that method of death before, many times. It was his eyes. They were wide open. Bright blue. Staring into space. His bushy white eyebrows were pushed high up his forehead. She had never seen the eyes remain open like that in a voluntary suicide. The plastic bag method was also known as the 'final exit' method, which involved sleeping pills and a bag over the head which might be tied at the bottom with a cord. The idea was to fall asleep peacefully and never wake up. Howard's surprised expression and staring eyes were more suggestive of a sudden, traumatic death.

She moved on to the photographs of Bea Ainsworth. Hurst was not easily shocked. Death was a common currency to her. She had spent many hours identifying bodies in the mortuary. But she was appalled by the level of violence on show. She flicked through the pages of Bea's post-mortem examination report. The autopsy had been conducted by Dr Alan Roy Williams, a Home Office Pathologist and Consultant Pathologist at Macclesfield Hospital. DS Woolley, DC Cantello, DC Warren and PC Bagley had been present. The officers informed Williams that Bea was found on the bed next to her husband. He was also told by the officers that a suicide note was discovered next to the bodies, and a 'large amount' of euthanasia material was present in the house. Bea had arrived at the hospital in a body bag with her head, hands and feet covered by plastic bags in order to preserve any forensic evidence. She was still wearing her white nightdress and fluffy light-brown socks.

Williams saw that her wounds were extensive, indicating a prolonged and sustained attack. Above her eye was a lacerated wound three inches long and three-quarters of an inch wide. At the centre of her forehead was an irregular triangular-shaped wound, with another wound just above her left eye. There was bruising on her left eyebrow and her left eyelid. Abrasions on both her knees and below the patella of each knee. Deep scratches on her right leg and bruises on her shin. A kitchen knife had been embedded into the central part of her forehead.

The knife had a wooden handle, with a blade-length measuring five-and-a-half inches. The blade featured a single cutting edge and had penetrated her left optic nerve, through the left side of the pons, and emerged into the posterior of the left cerebellum, the part of the brain responsible for co-ordinating voluntary movement, and motor skills such as balance and posture. She had extensive lacerated wounds across both frontal lobes, caused by repeated blows from a heavy blunt object, probably the washed-down hammer found in the bathroom sink. Bea's official cause of death was a combination of head injuries from the hammer and the final stab wound into the brain.

Howard's autopsy was carried out at 5 p.m. on the same day, also by Dr Williams. He was found to be of an average build. He had two bruises on his right upper lip and left upper lip. There was a scratch on his left knee. His body showed signs of rigor mortis, otherwise known as the stiffening of the body's muscles after death. Hypostasis, or the accumulation of blood due to gravity, was present in his back, which had turned a shade of deep purple. His scalp and skull showed no signs of bruising.

He had died from suffocation. Simply put, his airway had
been obstructed by the bag on his head which killed him. But
there was something which puzzled Williams, something
which didn't fit with the rest of the suicide narrative. In his
report to the detectives he could not explain how Howard had
got the bruises to his upper lips. They remained unexplained.
But Hurst had seen injuries like it before. They were common
marks in cases of asphyxiation. Marks caused, for example, by
a person clamping their hand around your mouth and nose to
stop you from breathing, by the lips being pressed against the
teeth, a soft surface against a hard one, hence the bruising.

Hurst returned to the crime scene photographs. Apart
from the obvious violence, there was another feature of Bea's
horrific death which caught her eye. Her nightdress had been
hitched up, exposing her pubic area. It was too high up her leg
to have simply ridden up by itself. Somebody had yanked up
her nightie. It was the ultimate indignity, and an action which
troubled Hurst. Why would Howard have done such a thing
to his wife? Why leave her exposed to the people who would
eventually find them? Did he hate her so much? Was her murder
partly about a desire to humiliate her? It seemed so out of character for such a gentle-seeming elderly couple.

Hurst mentioned her concerns to the detectives, and was
told by one male detective that the nightdress probably 'rode up
her leg' in the night while she was asleep. Hurst doubted that.
She had been a nurse in a hospital. She had plenty of experience
of dealing with patients and their nightdresses. The nightie was
far too high up for that. Even if the detective's hypothesis was
true, why would Howard murder Bea and leave her in such a
state? Hurst read in the file that the Ainsworths had a belief

in euthanasia. But the core principle of euthanasia was about achieving dignity in death. There was nothing dignified about the death of Bea Ainsworth. Quite the opposite.

Hurst saw the bottle of chlormethiazole pills on Howard's bedside dresser. She was familiar with the medication from when she had worked as a nurse. On the wards, those types of pills were used to help with sedation and sleep, or for dementia or confusion in the elderly. Hurst could find nothing in the Ainsworths' medical information to explain why they might need such a drug. Neither of them had any known history of dementia or confusion. Hurst contacted the Kenmore Medical Centre on Alderley Road in Wilmslow and spoke to one of the doctors at the practice. Neither Howard nor Bea, the doctor confirmed, had ever been prescribed such a medication. So where did the bottle of tablets come from? How had they got hold of this medication? And why hadn't Howard taken the tablets to aid his suicide method when he was so well versed in the final exit method?

Hurst's doubts were growing. She could find nothing in the Ainsworths' medical or social histories to indicate why Howard might want to murder Bea. But there was one telling detail in particular about the crime scene which Hurst couldn't get out of her mind. Where was the blood on Howard's pyjamas? Where was the blood on his hands and face? The photographs showed a couple of droplets on his top, while his wife, next to him, whom he had apparently just bludgeoned with a hammer and stabbed in the head with a kitchen knife, was bathed in blood. How could he have carried out such a sustained attack without getting more blood on him? The coroner would want to know how that was possible.

Hurst followed up with the SOCO who had carried out the majority of the evidence recovery work on Gravel Lane. 'I'm worried about the lack of blood stains on Howard's pyjamas,' she said. 'Were any other clothes with blood on them found in the house?'

'No,' he frowned. 'Nothing. It's a strange one.'

Hurst didn't think Howard had changed his clothes. She saw that his pyjamas were stained with dribbles, a sign they weren't freshly worn, something she would look out for in elderly patients during her days working on a ward. The SOCO said the house had been scrubbed clean for the arrival of John Ainsworth at 2.25 p.m. on the Monday afternoon. Hurst was shocked. Bea's post-mortem hadn't been until 3 p.m. that day and Howard's at 5 p.m. It meant the bedroom had been scrubbed of the evidence before the pathologist had even had a chance to examine the bodies. Hurst also claims she was told the hammer, knife and plastic bag had not been subject to fingerprinting tests at that time and was told so by the SOCO.

Hurst was about to criticise a murder inquiry, something possibly unprecedented for a coroner's officer in the county of Cheshire. She knew what most detectives would think: how can a coroner's officer with no policing background question a murder investigation? She had heard the whispers in the corridors – there goes little Miss Marple, poking her nose into cases that don't concern her . . . If it backfired, it could cost her career in the force. But deep down, she felt like something had been missed. She knew it was the right thing to do.

She had already devised a strategy. She would blame it on the coroner. She knew the police officers were frightened of Hibbert. Name-dropping Hibbert might give her the leverage she needed. She arranged a meeting with her superintendent, who was the liaison between the police and coroner's office. He was new in the job, with a respectful, approachable manner about him, and Hurst felt he was the sort of police officer who might listen to her concerns rather than dismiss them.

She met him in his office at the station and raised the issue of the knife, hammers and plastic bag not being tested for fingerprints. 'I'm afraid the coroner might ask why.' She urged him to ask for more testing to be carried out. The superintendent seemed concerned by what he was hearing. He assured Hurst he would look into the matter, and she left his office feeling satisfied she had done the right thing.

But behind the scenes, police investigators were convinced that Howard was the killer. There was a suicide letter. His belief in euthanasia. No sign of forced entry. Besides, who knows what goes on behind closed doors? To the outside world, they may have appeared a devoted elderly couple, but indoors they might have rowed like cats and dogs. The most likely explanation based on the evidence at hand was that Howard had murdered Bea and taken his own life in the mistaken belief that Bea was not going to recover from her minor ailment. It had to be him. Surely.

4

Death Without Dignity

After the Ainsworths' bodies were discovered, the Wilmslow detectives set about interviewing family, friends and neighbours to build up a profile of Howard and Bea. They wanted to know their motivations, desires and, most importantly, any skeletons lurking in their past which might explain their unusually violent deaths. It was all standard procedure for a murder investigation.

One line of enquiry they were eager to explore more fully was the couple's belief in euthanasia. Jacqueline Cummings, the neighbour who had lived next door with her husband Halton since 1977, had an interesting story to tell on the matter. Some fifteen years earlier, Howard had knocked on their door and presented a document to Jacqueline. He wanted her to witness his signature. 'I believe in euthanasia,' Howard told her frankly. 'I don't believe in keeping people alive with drugs.'

Rather taken aback by Howard's declaration, Jacqueline nevertheless invited him in. She remembered him being quite forceful in his views. As far as Jacqueline could tell, Howard and Bea were in perfectly good health, and at that time euthanasia appeared to be a consideration for the distant future: a back-up plan in case one of them deteriorated and the other was unable to cope. Neither of them could stand the thought of going into a care home. It was not something Howard or Bea could ever contemplate doing.

Despite her unease, Jacqueline signed the papers. She would later have doubts about whether she had done the right thing. When interviewed by the detectives, Jacqueline gave them her honest view of their relationship. 'I got the impression regarding their devotion to each other that he couldn't live without her,' she said. 'They seemed to do everything and go everywhere together.'

She told the police about the minor row with Howard and Bea when they had had an extension to their house built. In the lead-up to their deaths, she hadn't seen Bea for several weeks. She had seen Howard a few days before their bodies were found. She couldn't be certain what day, but she'd spotted him one morning through the window of his kitchen. He appeared to be acting normally. Nothing out of the ordinary that she could report.

The police delved further into Howard and Bea's euthanasia beliefs, and their enquiries led them to the Scottish Voluntary Euthanasia Society (SVES), also known as EXIT, a non-profit organisation funded by public donations, membership, book sales and legacies which had broken away from the wider UK organisation in 1980 in order to publish the booklet *How to Die with Dignity*. SVES wanted legal reform to make euthanasia an option available to anyone in the UK.

They contacted Christopher Docker, the executive secretary, at SVES's headquarters in Edinburgh, and on Thursday, 27 June 1996, he was visited there by DC Paton from the Lothian and Borders police, who told him about the police inquiry in Cheshire relating to the deaths of Howard and Bea Ainsworth. Docker checked his records and confirmed the couple had indeed joined the group on 20 June 1990 and had life membership status. They had pre-paid for a copy of *How to Die with Dignity* which had been posted out and stamped with with the unique number 3209. The couple had made financial contributions of £114 and had recently become supporters of SVES, paying an additional fee of £50 per year, receiving a quarterly newsletter and a bi-annual circular from the charity.

Docker explained how the Ainsworths would have signed up to the charity. A membership application would be received in the post on one of its pre-formatted application forms, which were distributed widely. The details given on the form would be transferred onto the computer database and the form then destroyed. SVES would wait three months before sending any literature at all to the new member, and then in order to receive *How to Die with Dignity* the Ainsworths would have had to make a further request. Docker thought they may also have received a copy of the supplement to *How to Die with Dignity*. The booklets provided advice on depression, legal warnings and considerations regarding next of kin, and also gave advice on methods of suicide, including the methods which the society staunchly opposed. It was against the use of knives in any way in the act of euthanasia.

Docker was told that Howard had taken his life by use of a plastic bag. The plastic bag method was well documented in *How to Die with Dignity*, said Docker. Although most people who purchased the booklet would never make use of its contents, those who had read it would know that sedative drugs should be used in conjunction with a plastic bag. Docker said he was surprised that Howard had not taken the sedatives: in his experience, when pills were not used, the person was likely to simply thrash about and then pull the bag from their head at the very last moment. No matter how much somebody wants to die, when desperation kicks in, the human instinct to survive will always look for an escape.

Howard would have known that tablets were part of the final exit method. Indeed, he had even written down the exact method in a note found in the sitting room by DS Woolley. There were sedatives lying in a bottle on the bedside table on Howard's side of the bed: twenty-two brown-and-grey tablets which would have eased his suffering considerably.

While Docker could understand Howard's method of euthanasia, even if it did miss out a vital step, he was utterly horrified by the way Bea had died. He made it clear to Paton: none of the literature produced by SVES would *ever* encourage taking your own life or the life of another in such a way. He described it as a 'strange and illegal act', and said he was 'shocked by it'. When seeking 'self-deliverance', the group's members wanted quiet, dignified, non-violent deaths which caused the minimum amount of distress to those who found their bodies. That was the whole point of euthanasia and the right to choose. Bea had had no choice in her death.

Despite the issues thrown up by Docker, police still had the suicide letter. As part of their enquiries, DS Woolley's team had contacted a handwriting expert for advice about the suicide note purportedly written by Howard. Paul Rimmer, who worked for Document Evidence Limited in Birmingham, had more than twenty years of experience in examining documents and handwriting of unknown or disputed origin and was used as an expert witness in court cases. Rimmer was provided with five samples of handwriting: the handwritten note found in the bedroom with John's address and contact details; the suicide note; the note about Bea's symptoms; the message at the top of the stairs which said **DO NOT RESUCACATE**; and the note found in the sitting room which described a possible suicide method.

Against those samples, Rimmer was then provided with 'specimen' samples of Howard's handwriting, from an Abbey National 'Tessa' application, a diary, a piece of card, two pieces of paper and an insurance letter. In Rimmer's opinion, the handwriting in the samples was fluently written and matched the handwriting in the confirmed specimens. Rimmer concluded that Howard was the author of the notes found in the house, including the suicide note.

Meanwhile, detectives had submitted a number of items for forensic testing to the Forensic Science Service (FSS) at Chorley Laboratory in Washington Hall, one of seven laboratories the FSS had at the time in England and Wales. The FSS was government-owned and provided forensic science services to police forces until its final closure in 2012, when the government decided to transfer operations to the private sector to save money, a move heavily criticised in Parliament. The items handed over to the FSS included the ballpein hammer in the main bedroom, the hammer from the bathroom sink and the knife found in Bea's forehead. The lab tested blood swabs taken from Howard's and Bea's bodies, and a swab from Howard's right hand to see if Bea's blood was on it. Officers also asked the scientists to check if a hammer had been used to strike the butt of the knife when it was placed against Bea's forehead.

The report from the laboratory was sent to Cheshire Police on 16 July 1996. Philip Rydeard, a forensic scientist employed by the FSS, had carried out an examination of the knife and found no evidence that the wooden handle had been struck by the hammer or any other heavy item. In view of that finding, he did not then examine the hammers themselves.

Christine Hurst, who was eagerly awaiting the results, was informed by officers on the inquiry team that the tests on the knife and hammer had been inconclusive. It could not be established whether Howard had held either of the weapons. The plastic bag had proved too contaminated for fingerprint tests to be conducted: by the time the knife, hammer and plastic bag had been handed over to the laboratory, Hurst was told, too many people had handled them. Nevertheless, the police remained confident Howard was the killer because of the suicide letter that had been found in the bedroom. But couldn't a letter be faked? Or written under duress?

There was one last avenue Hurst could pursue in order to raise her concerns. She worked for Cheshire Police, but under the direction and guidance of the senior coroner for the county of Cheshire. The coroner, James Hibbert, was her ultimate line manager. She had pushed the police into conducting more forensics tests on the murder weapons, but these had been handled so many times they were evidentially useless. She had raised her concerns about the case with senior officers. She thought long and hard about raising her issues with Hibbert himself. She never did. In the years to come, it would remain a matter of personal regret.

The police investigation was wound down, and on 12 July 1996 DS Woolley wrote a report for the attention of his

supervisor, Chief Inspector Wilson. 'From the evidence contained in this file it is the conclusion of the reporting officer
that Howard Ainsworth killed his wife by hitting her head
with a hammer and then stabbing her through the brain before
committing suicide by suffocation,' wrote Woolley. 'I forward
this report for your information.'

Three months later, at Warrington coroner's court, John
Finlay Hibbert presided over an inquest into the deaths of the
Ainsworths. Hibbert had been a coroner in Cheshire since 1958
when he was just thirty years old, becoming the youngest coroner since records began. He would later retire in 1999, having
officiated over a number of high-profile inquests, including the
victims of the Winsford train disaster in 1962, when eighteen
people died after the train driver went through a stop signal;
the children killed in the Warrington bomb attack by the IRA
in 1993; and the death of Chelsea Football Club vice-chairman
Matthew Harding in a helicopter crash near Middlewich in
Cheshire while flying back from a Bolton Wanderers match.

Hibbert considered evidence from DS Woolley, Margaret
Farror and John Ainsworth, and at the end of the hearing,
guided by the evidence provided to him by the police inquiry,
recorded that Howard took his own life, while Bea was unlawfully killed. As far as the police and coroner were concerned,
it was case closed.

The case may have been shut down, but it was not forgotten.
Not by everyone. Hurst placed the Ainsworths' files in a box
in her office marked 'Special Interest', which over the years
would collect other mysterious deaths from across the county.
She wanted to make sure she had a record of the case to hand.

One day, she hoped, somebody might re-investigate those killings, and prove what she suspected all along: that Howard was innocent, and the real killer had got away with it.

The story of the Ainsworths might have ended there. But then, three years later, a few streets away from the Ainsworths' home in Gravel Lane, a second elderly couple were found dead in their bloodstained bed, lying side by side in their nightclothes, bodies ripped and torn, the woman's nightdress yanked up to expose her pubic area. This time the police suspected a killer was on the loose. And they launched a hunt to catch him.

5

The Wards

On the Cheshire plain between the River Bollin and River Dean, the sleepy town of Wilmslow sits amid green fields, a sharp break from the amorphous sprawl creeping from the suburbs of south Manchester. Wilmslow's ready water supply and fuel from the local peat bogs has ensured its survival as a settlement down the centuries. These days it is regarded one of the wealthiest areas in the UK outside of London. Its commutable distance to Manchester United's and Manchester City's stadiums and training grounds has made the town popular with footballers keen to live outside Manchester in order to maintain some semblance of privacy. Sir Alex Ferguson, the legendary former United manager, lives in a gated mansion close to the railway station and is occasionally seen eating lunch in a Turkish café in the town centre. Bill Roache, who plays Ken Barlow in *Coronation Street*, is another famous resident. Many of the scenes from the TV reality soap opera *The Real Housewives of Cheshire* are shot in Wilmslow, and one of its stars, Tanya Bardsley, married to footballer Phil Bardsley, has a 'health, wellness and positivity' boutique on the high street. Supercars are a common enough sight in the streets: Lamborghinis, Ferraris, Aston Martins, Porsches. At the weekends they sit in shiny rows outside wine bars, while their owners sit at tables along the pavements, giving parts of the town an almost continental feel.

The perceived wealth and decadent lifestyle of some of Wilmslow's inhabitants has come with the criticism that parts of the community have become superficial and money-orientated. A former vicar of St Bartholomew's, where the Ainsworths' funeral service had been held, once wrote in the parish magazine that Wilmslow's residents were 'as pagan as any group of people I have ever met'. The article, published at the end of the Revd David Leaver's tenure at the church, accused the community of being materialistic, obsessed with money and removed from spiritual values. 'In this part of north Cheshire meets south Manchester suburbs, the question seems essentially materialistic: "How much money do you earn? What car do you drive? How big is your house?" I have never', wrote Leaver, 'met people who are quite so obsessed with money.'

Undoubtably there is wealth in Wilmslow. But not everybody is a millionaire. Many of its residents are hard-working professionals who want to raise their families in a town with a low rate of violent crime, good schools and plenty of green space. Wards like Lacey Green feature the same deprivation and poverty you will find in any town or city in England, but there is a pride in being a resident of Wilmslow, an acknowledgement among the people who sit at the tables of its restaurants and coffee bars that they have 'done well' in life to be able to live there, and that their children will be raised in an environment where they will be safe and have every opportunity to make something of themselves.

The town itself has a population of around 30,000, but still manages to maintain a village-like atmosphere. People in

Wilmslow know one another. They stop and talk as they stroll down Grove Street or Water Lane on a sunny day, heading to the Carrs to walk the dog, or to the Waitrose down the hill. The older ladies and gentlemen who meet one other in the café at the top of Hoopers department store know one another's business, and gossip about the love affairs of friends, grand houses bought and sold, the careers of their children and the private schools of their grandchildren.

In November 1999, one of the main topics of gossip was Sally Clark, a corporate solicitor with the Manchester-based law firm Addleshaw Booth, who owned a £300,000 cottage with her husband on South Oak Lane, which joins on to Gravel Lane, where the Ainsworths once lived. Clark had just been found guilty of murdering her two infant children. Chester Crown Court heard evidence that she had smothered her eleven-week-old son Christopher while her husband was at his office Christmas party, then thirteen months later shaken his eight-week-old brother Harry to death.

Clark was portrayed by the police and prosecution as a 'lonely drunk' who had resented her children for keeping her away from her well-paid job. She was locked up in Styal women's prison, just up the road on the other side of the Carrs. On her first day she was attacked by a fellow inmate and left with black eyes after being smashed in the face with a plastic mug. It took more than three years to overturn her conviction, after the prosecution was found to have relied upon flawed evidence which seriously misled the jury, rendering the conviction unsafe. The case would later be described as a stain on the reputation of Cheshire Police and the British legal system. She died in 2007 at the age of forty-two from acute alcohol poisoning.

But Sally Clark was not the only topic of conversation for the well-dressed ladies at the tables of Hoopers' café. An elderly couple called Donald and Auriel Ward had been found stabbed to death in the bedroom of their large bungalow. The police had tents up outside the house. TV and newspaper reporters were canvassing neighbours, trying to learn anything they could about the murdered couple. Word was spreading through Wilmslow like wildfire. *A killer was on the loose.*

Lacey Grove was a cul-de-sac pocketed between some of the quieter residential streets of Wilmslow. The narrow entrance off Lacey Green was easy to miss, even for pedestrians walking past. The cul-de-sac was a nowhere space, a patch of land somehow dropped in between the other streets, hemmed in by trees, bushes and the backs of other people's houses. Many had lived in the neighbourhood for decades without being aware of its existence. There were just three large houses on the road, each of them with substantial gardens. At night the road was pitch black and eerily quiet. There were no streetlamps.

The paper boys used to dread going up that road in the early hours. David Sydenham had delivered papers to that street at the age of thirteen. Grown up now with children of his own, with a job as a crane operator building skyscrapers in Manchester city centre, Sydenham remembers Lacey Grove all too well: the looming bushes and trees rising either side of the cave-like entrance. At six o'clock in the morning in winter, as he clutched his bag of papers, walking down that entrance felt like entering the dark mouth of a monster.

The first house on the right belonged to Roger Bugler, a retired civil engineer and Cambridge graduate. In the next house along was Wendy Smith, an NHS nurse with two teen-age children who had moved to Wilmslow in 1997. She was the newest arrival in Lacey Grove. Then, at the bottom of the street, past a thick clutch of rhododendron bushes, was the third and final house: No.3, Lacey Grove.

In November 1999, the house belonged to Donald and Auriel Ward, a couple aged seventy-three and sixty-eight respectively, who were enjoying a well-earned retirement, going on regular driving trips around Europe, watching their local orchestra perform once a week in Manchester, and spending time with their children and grandchildren, for whom they would drop everything to go and help whenever they were needed. The Wards were selfless when it came to family. Nothing was more important than their grandchildren, and they played an active role in their lives, babysitting when asked, and watching them perform in countless school plays and concerts.

Donald was a research chemist at the Central Electricity Generating Board (CEGB), while Auriel had been a nursery school leader. They had raised three sons, Michael, David and Simon. They'd settled in Wilmslow in Lacey Grove in 1969, a house which came with a third of an acre of land. By 1999, Simon was living in a house in Stockport with his own family, working as a psychiatric nurse in Heaton Moor. Michael was a chartered accountant in Staffordshire, and David a manager with Sainsbury's in West Sussex.

Donald had raised his children in a disciplined manner, dominating their lives into early adulthood. He was proud of his sons and how well they had done in their careers, and would often boast about them to Roger next door: Michael was doing this, David was doing that. He was an educated and intelligent man, a fellow of the Royal Institute of Chemists with two degrees, but had stopped working as a research chemist at the CEGB after suffering a heart attack and decided to take retirement at the age of sixty-three. He kept his mind active by keeping up to date with current affairs and forensically reading the daily newspapers delivered by young Sydenham from the newsagents around the corner. He would send his son, Simon, any news clippings he found about clinical psychiatry.

Donald's other great love was classical music. The Wards had a season ticket for the Hallé, Manchester's symphony orchestra, which puts on around seventy concerts a year in the Bridgewater Hall, opposite the Midland Hotel in Manchester city centre, and would usually attend on a Wednesday or a Thursday. They had seen Puccini's *Tosca*, Mark Elder conducting the first Manchester performance of Anthony Payne's reconstruction of Elgar's Symphony No. 3, and the orchestra's centenary concert. Donald would dress smartly for the occasion – shirt and a jacket. He had silver wavy hair, brushed left to right, slightly receded. At five feet nine he was much shorter than the likes of Howard Ainsworth, with a smaller frame. He weighed just over ten stone, and had lost weight in the years following his heart attack.

He kept fit by walking at least two miles most mornings, heading into Wilmslow down Cliff Road, past the Carrs on his right and over the River Bollin, dressed in his trilby hat and beige jacket and looking like a character out of *Brighton Rock*. He was learning French and had a number of French pen pals to help him practise. Some of his friends thought it was to impress Auriel when they went away to Europe on one of their road trips.

When it came to his wife he was regarded as a romantic. He was always treating her on their wedding anniversary to a trip away, usually the Lake District, and at weekends they would visit places like Alderley Edge and Tatton Park, a large manor hall where deer roam freely in the acres of green fields. He was caring towards her. If he ever saw Auriel in the garden, chatting to their neighbour, Wendy, over the fence, he would come out to drape a cardigan over her shoulders.

Like most people, of course, he was far from perfect. He could be known for being rather pernickety. Dogmatic. Stubborn. The sort of person who always thought he was in the right, and liked people to know it. Auriel was forever apologising for him. But those who knew him best would simply roll their eyes: it was just 'Donald being Donald'. Auriel was a little more laid-back than her husband. She was the perfect foil, and she loved him dearly.

Auriel was a small lady, and at five feet four inches was half a head shorter than her husband. She had short, dark, slightly curly hair, wore spectacles, and her green-brown eyes carried a touch of mischief about them, especially when she was poking fun at her slightly pretentious husband. She was a keen gardener, and the two of them would put in an equal share of work on their large plot. Popular with her friends and neighbours, she was known for her good sense of humour: she had a glide in one eye she could be a little self-conscious about – 'When I'm talking to the shop assistant,' she would jokingly complain to the women in Salon Pampas hairdressers, run by her friend Mary Colborn-Roberts, 'they always think I'm looking at someone else.'

Auriel visited the salon every Thursday for her weekly hair

appointment, where there would be endless talk about her sons and grandchildren. Mary had heard it all when it came to the gossip of Cheshire. Marriages, affairs, break-ups – everything would be divulged in that roomful of ladies wielding scissors and hairdryers. Salon Pampas was like the town's unofficial confessional.

But Auriel never had a bad word to say about her Donald. Not in all the years Mary knew her: in fact, quite the opposite. They were happily married. Indeed, Auriel was the sort who would fret about everyone else around her – Simon might need this, Michael will want that. It was a running joke among her friends that Auriel worried about every single person in her life except herself. Auriel, Mary would often say, was a 'lady of her time'. She was quiet but quick-witted, a woman of consistent mood whose focus, attentions and interests were concentrated outwards.

The Wards led comfortable lives. Money wasn't an issue: the house was paid off, while their estate, in today's money, was worth about £700,000. Money was paid every month from Donald's CEGB pension. A new car was always on the driveway. Every five or six weeks, the Wards packed up the car and took off on holiday across Europe. Donald would do most of the driving, and could be critical of his wife's abilities behind the wheel.

In 1999, they hadn't gone on holiday after having been involved in a nasty car accident in Derbyshire. They had been on a trip to the Peak District when their SUV was in a crash near Castleton. They had to be cut free by the emergency services and their car was written off. The accident left Auriel badly shaken, but Donald played it down, telling his sons it was 'nothing' and 'no big deal'. Donald didn't like people making a fuss. He would conceal his limitations. If anybody offered to help him carry something heavy he'd say, 'It's not heavy, it's just an awkward shape.'

Like the Ainsworths, the Wards were fiercely independent and rarely asked their children for any help. They wanted to help their sons with the grandchildren, not be a burden themselves. They remembered how tough it could be to raise a family. Donald was fiercely protective: when the grandchildren came to visit, they would sometimes play outside on roller skates and scooters, and Donald would put out a handmade road sign which read: 'Caution – children playing'. His signs were a source of some amusement to their neighbours, Wendy and Roger. There were never any cars on their road. But that didn't stop Donald, who had a particular soft spot for Simon's daughter, Rosalyn. In his eyes Rosalyn could do no wrong, and he would wrap her up in cotton wool if he could.

Donald and Auriel had a set morning routine. They would wake at 6.30 a.m. Donald would go downstairs in his dressing gown, brew two teas and bring them back up to their bedroom on the first floor. He was a light sleeper and would often wake up if he 'heard a noise' and go downstairs to check, just in case. Ten years earlier they had been burgled and the house had been left in a mess. The Wards had never forgotten the experience. The intrusion. The sense that their private space had been invaded. Afterwards, the insurance company had insisted they get an alarm fitted.

They had also had a number of incidents with prowlers. Living on a secluded street made them more vulnerable. One day they were working in the front garden and went back inside the house to find a bedroom window at the back had been smashed. Again, it was unsettling. They had a separate alarm fitted to the back bedroom door, just in case.

Donald was the co-ordinator of the local Neighbourhood Watch scheme, and in the weeks leading up to his death was aware of a number of burglaries in the surrounding streets. Their children had grown increasingly worried about their relative isolation on Lacey Grove. It was so dark without any street lighting: a burglar or intruder could easily slip up the street in the dead of night and nobody would see a thing. More than once, Simon had raised the possibility of his parents moving out of their bungalow into something smaller, more manageable and less tucked away. They wouldn't hear of it. Nothing could persuade them to move out of the house they had lived in for the last thirty years. This was where they had raised their children. It meant something more than just bricks and mortar.

There was nothing curious or strange about the last days of Donald and Auriel Ward. They visited shops, had their front driveway resurfaced, paid minor bills, made plans to watch one of their grandchildren perform in a concert, arranged to babysit for Simon, invited Michael and his family to spend Christmas with them in Wilmslow. It was business as usual.

The new flagging on the driveway was a considerable investment for the future. They were always doing bits and pieces to keep the bungalow in good condition. A few years back they had spent thousands of pounds getting all the double glazing refitted. James Allen, a local handyman, had been recommended for some work on their driveway by their neighbour Wendy after he'd done a good job of building a mini-basketball court for her two children.

On the morning of Monday, 8 November 1999, Allen began work resurfacing the wide driveway at the front of the Wards' home. He would witness up close the interaction between Donald and Auriel in the days leading up to their deaths, making him a useful witness to the police investigation. Unfortunately, it would also make him a potential suspect in their murders, simply because he was one of the last people to see them alive. He was completely cleared of any involvement in their deaths, but given the choice, the weeks of late November, early December 1999 were a time Allen would rather scrub from his memory.

On Friday, 19 November, Allen was outside the house talking to Donald when it started to rain. The two men got on well. Allen regarded Donald as being 'polite and particular', with a sense of humour. Auriel saw that Donald was getting wet and cold, so she hurried outside with a coat to put around his shoulders. Shortly afterwards, Auriel joined their conversation. Donald took off his coat and wrapped it around her, preferring to be cold himself. It was Auriel's sixty-eighth birthday, and they were planning to celebrate properly the following day over lunch with their son Simon and his family. The touching moment in the pouring rain would stick in Allen's head. It wasn't hard to see they had a deep affection for one another.

The next day, Donald and Auriel met Simon, his wife June and their daughters Rosalyn and Phoebe for afternoon lunch at the Bridge Hotel in Prestbury, known for miles around for its excellent roast dinners. During lunch, Simon, who was thirty-nine at the time, saw his father's right hand was bandaged. Donald said he had been trying to change a lightbulb when it smashed. Wendy next door, who was a nurse, had put the dressing on. 'It's just a scratch,' Donald said, shrugging off his son and daughter-in-law's concern. 'Nothing serious.'

Simon and June gave Auriel her birthday presents: an umbrella and some M&S vouchers. Donald paid for lunch. The family left the Bridge Hotel in good spirits and headed back to Lacey Grove to continue Auriel's birthday celebrations. Auriel drove the six miles back to Wilmslow, Donald grumbling for most of the way and generally being a back-seat driver. Donald's moaning about her driving grated on Auriel, but over the years she had got used to it. He was never going to change.

Back at the house, the family discussed plans for Christmas. Michael and his wife were coming over for Christmas dinner. Donald and Auriel also made arrangements with Simon to watch Rosalyn perform in a concert on 10 December. The Wards agreed to babysit for their grandchildren on the 18th, which was a Saturday. It was life as normal for the Ward family. Nothing out of the ordinary. Nothing especially unusual. Auriel's birthday cake came out. Donald had trouble lighting the candles and singed his fingertips – he didn't have the same dexterity he had as a younger man. But that was just one of those things. The Wards didn't resent getting older. They were happy. They had their family, a nice house and enough money that they didn't have to worry.

On Monday, 22 November, Donald walked into the newsagents on Dean Row Road. He chatted to the owner, Susan Nobes, and paid his newspaper bill up until Saturday. Later on, the Wards went walking in Macclesfield Forest, one of their favourite spots and the last remnant of the Royal Forest of Macclesfield, an ancient hunting ground that once ran from the foothills of the Pennines to the Staffordshire moors, where red deer still roam among hundreds of hectares of Japanese larch, Sitka spruce, oak, sycamore, Corsican pine, Norway spruce and beech.

Afterwards the Wards did some shopping in Congleton, Mow Cop and Poynton. They bought a few things in Boots in Poynton and filled the car up at the Poynton Texaco before returning home at 3 p.m. Allen saw them arrive. He was finishing the driveway and returned his set of keys. The Wards seemed their usual happy selves. Donald asked Allen for the final bill, and Allen promised he would let him know as soon as he got home. Later that day Allen rang to say Donald owed a final payment of £785 for the driveway. At 7 p.m. Auriel spoke to one of her grandsons, Daniel, on the telephone, and they chatted about what Daniel was planning for his birthday and what he might want his grandparents to get him for Christmas. Auriel's conversation with her grandson was the final outgoing call made from the Wards' house.

It was Tuesday morning now. Allen received his cheque through the post from Donald, accompanied by a touching handwritten letter thanking him for his hard work and saying how pleased they were with their new driveway, and how much of an improvement it made to the front of the house. Allen banked it the same day.

At 10 a.m., Donald was due to check in his Renault Megane for a service at the Renault dealership in Altrincham. He never showed up. On Wednesday, Allen was back on Lacey Grove cutting Roger Bugler's hedgerows and repairing Wendy's carport gutter. He noticed one of the gates to the Wards' home was open. *Strange*, he thought. Donald was usually so security-conscious: he could be quite particular about shutting and locking the doors and gates to the house. Allen didn't see either of the Wards that day.

On Thursday morning at 9.30 Auriel was booked for her usual weekly appointment at Salon Pampas. She had set aside three hours to get a full perm with Mary, and also arranged to meet her friend Constance Boulton there and promised to give her a lift to Manchester Airport later that week – they'd agree the time while they were at the hairdresser's. Except Auriel never turned up. It wasn't like her to forget an appointment. If she ever had to cancel, she'd always call Mary to let her know.

Mary was worried. The appointment was for a full perm – a big one to miss. She didn't believe it was something Auriel would just forget about, unless there was a family emergency. She telephoned the Wards' house. No answer. She tried several more times that day. Nothing. Constance went to Lacey Grove and knocked on the door. No reply. She put a note through the letterbox, written by Mary, saying 'Sorry about the missed appointment' and 'Hope you are okay'. When Constance posted the note she noticed a pile of post and letters on the other side – the sort of pile you might expect to find after returning from holiday.

By now the Ward family was also getting worried. Simon would normally get a phone call from his mother or father on Tuesday evening. Neither had rung. He rang the house on Wednesday evening. No answer. On Thursday his brother Michael tried. Nothing. Simon tried again on Friday, but again, nobody picked up. Simon decided it was time for further action. He telephoned Michael's wife, Gillian, who got in touch with her father Stanley Martlew, who lived in Wilmslow. Just before 5 p.m. that day, Stanley arrived at Lacey Grove and knocked on the door of No. 3. There was no reply. He tried Wendy Smith's house.

'I've been sent round by the family,' he explained when Wendy came to the door. 'They haven't been in touch with anyone for the last four days. Have you got a key?'

Wendy said she didn't, but that Roger next door had one. Stanley called on Roger, explained himself, and Roger said he would go with him, even though he had guests round. Roger was a close friend of the Wards and was concerned by the news that they hadn't been in touch with the family for so long. Come to think of it, he couldn't remember seeing Donald or Auriel for a good few days.

The two men walked up the Wards' driveway. Roger tried the kitchen door. It was closed but unlocked. That was strange, he thought: Donald would always keep the doors locked, even when they were pottering about in the front garden. They went through into the kitchen. The table was set for breakfast, but there were no dirty plates in the sink. The Wards didn't use their front door and had blocked it off a while ago with furniture. Beneath the letterbox were Donald's newspapers, delivered faithfully each day by Sydenham, in chronological order as they had fallen: at the very bottom was Tuesday's, then Wednesday's, Thursday's, and Friday's was top of the pile – all untouched, just as they had landed. By now Roger was seriously worried. Donald would read the paper every single day, cover to cover. And if they had gone on holiday, why had they left the kitchen door unlocked?

Roger entered the security code into the alarm to find the system had already been deactivated. The system used infrared sensors on all the rooms inside the house, along with magnetic sensors on the rear and kitchen doors. The two ground-floor bedrooms had independent alarm sensors. Friends used to joke that the Wards' house was like Fort Knox, they had so many alarms and locks. The two men checked the downstairs and found nothing out of place. Everything was as it should be, except there was no sign of Donald or Auriel.

Mystified, they went upstairs and into the main bedroom. The room was dark. They turned on the light to find Donald and Auriel lying dead in bed. Donald's throat had been cut. They could see the handle of a knife sticking out of his chest. Auriel, next to him, was staring up at the ceiling, her neck covered in stab marks. On top of her was a heap of white sheets topped with a pink woollen blanket. There was blood everywhere – on the mattress, the bedsheets, the pillows. A pillow placed against Auriel's face was now stained deep pink.

The two men backed out of the bedroom and down the stairs, utterly stunned by what they had just seen. It then occurred to them that the attacker could still be in the house. They left, quickly. Back inside Roger's house, Roger called 999. The time was now 5.01 p.m. After alerting the emergency services, Roger decided he had better let Wendy know what was going on. After all, at the time she was living alone with her two children, and there could well be a maniac on the loose. Her eleven-year-old son answered the door, and Roger asked to speak to his mother. When Wendy appeared in the hallway she could see from Roger's face that something was terribly wrong.

'We found Donald and Auriel,' he said. 'They're dead. You don't need to go inside. There's nothing you can do for them now. Police are on their way.'

'They're *dead*? But . . . how? What happened?'

Roger paused. He glanced to his left, towards the Wards' house, scanning the front windows, just in case he saw a curtain flicker. His mind was struggling to compute what his eyes had just seen. 'They've been murdered,' he told Wendy, as the sirens grew louder.

6

Hunting a Killer

PC Craig Lindfield was the first police officer to arrive at Lacey Grove. Slightly balding, with an accent straight from *Corrie*, he was a uniformed constable at the time but would later go on to have a long career as a detective, and in all those years to come he would never forget what he saw inside the Wards' bedroom. Coppers back then were supposed to take the 'stiff upper lip' approach: by all means, go for a pint with the lads at the station, but then put it behind you and get on with the next job. Except as a police officer you find there are some cases that never leave you: crimes that stay in the memory long after the case files are closed. For Lindfield this was one such case.

Lindfield went into the house with Roger Bugler, who showed him upstairs to the bedroom. He inspected the bodies and noticed on the bedsheets several broken pieces of light-brown pottery. He saw no sign of forced entry. Nothing appeared to have been stolen from the bedroom – a money belt was in plain view. Lindfield sealed the house and radioed the control room for back-up, providing a brief summary of what he had found. The cogs were starting to turn. Word was starting to trickle up the ranks of Cheshire police force: a wealthy elderly couple had been found dead in their house in Wilmslow, and it looked like a double murder.

Later that evening, Home Office pathologist Dr Paul Johnson arrived at Wilmslow Police Station, where he met Detective Superintendent Hood and Detective Inspector Birt to be briefed on the known facts of the case. Elderly couple. No records of domestic violence. Both kept in regular touch with their family. They had stopped answering their house phone, which had led the family to investigate, and they had been discovered dead at around 5 p.m.

Johnson and Hood arrived at Lacey Grove just after 10 p.m. In the bedroom Johnson began an examination of the scene. From the doorway he could see a window on the wall opposite, and a writing bureau and dressing table to his left, where there was a cupboard close to the door. The double bed was to the right. On Auriel's side of the bed was a table with a landline telephone (handset and receiver) and a silver portable radio.

The Wards were left as they had been found: the officers were under strict instructions not to touch anything before the pathologist and forensics team had examined the room so as not to contaminate any potential evidence. Johnson stood at the end of the bed, facing the headboard. Auriel was on the right, square on her back, head leaning back a touch, exposing the wounds on her neck. Her eyes were closed, skin glossy and yellow. Her mouth was hanging open in a half-moon shape; her short hair was lank and matted with blood. Her pyjamas were stained pink from blood and rucked open at the chest. A bloodstained pillow was resting against her left cheek.

Johnson saw straight away the obvious damage to her neck, head and face. Blood from the wounds had seeped into the mattress. Draped over her body was a pink woollen blanket. On top of the bed and at her sides were shards from a broken ceramic hot-water bottle — the Wards owned a big white pot which they filled with boiling water and placed in their bed to warm it up before they got in. Even in 1999, ceramic hot-water bottles would be considered museum pieces.

Donald's body was twisted to one side, with his head and neck turned up towards the ceiling. His left arm was reaching towards Auriel, his hand resting on the pillow close to her head. His right arm was draped across his front, up against his neck. Under his right arm, a knife handle was sticking out of the centre of his chest. His pillow was red and thick with congealed blood, apart from the top section of the pillow, which was still white. The fabric in the centre of the pillow appeared to be riddled with stab and slash marks.

The SOCOs had made themselves busy taking footage and photographs of the house and the bedroom. The Wards' deaths were certified by Dr Caprio, the same police surgeon who had attended the Ainsworth's home three years earlier. Johnson got to work. He directed the SOCOs to gently lift the bedclothes covering Donald and Auriel. Underneath, her nightie had been pulled high to her waist, exposing her pubic area. A second knife was found in the twisted bundle of blankets, the blade nineteen centimetres long with a serrated cutting edge. The knife was bloodstained. Auriel's body was cold to the touch. Her body was stiff and the skin on her face had tightened. Rigor mortis had set in. Johnson saw the blanket on the left side of her body appeared to be tucked in, almost as though somebody had been making her comfortable before bedtime.

The police team worked through the night. SOCOs placed plastic bags over Donald and Auriel's heads, hands and feet to preserve their bodies for the post-mortem examination.

Undertakers from Albert R. Slack, Bea Ainsworth's old employer, arrived in Lacey Grove to transport the bodies to the mortuary at Macclesfield General Hospital.

Johnson began Donald's autopsy in the early hours of Saturday morning. Present for the post-mortem were Detective Superintendent Hood, SOCO supervisor Hugh Owen, Melanie Barlow, another SOCO, Detective Constable Hughes, Detective Constable Hever, Detective Constable Walsh and Detective Constable Birchall. Cheshire Police's top brass were taking no chances. They had heard about the multiple slashes on Donald's hands — cuts that looked very much like defence wounds, as if he had been trying to protect himself from somebody wielding a sharp object, most probably a knife. There was also an injury to his mouth which could have come from an assault.

The wounds inflicted on Donald's body depicted a horrifying level of violence. Across Donald's upper neck, just above his Adam's apple, was a deep slice measuring 13cm, gaping to a width of 3cm, along with a smaller wound of 3cm on his neck. The wounds had cut into an internal jugular vein. This was regarded as a mortal wound, meaning the injury would have been enough to kill him, probably within seconds. But the injuries did not stop there.

A knife had been inserted into Donald's chest, penetrating below his fourth rib, slicing the intercostal muscle adjacent to the breastbone and entering his heart. He had stab wounds to his groin, a wound on his left elbow, wounds to his wrist, and damage to his left thumb and the tip of his left middle finger. On the palm of his right hand was a deep cut, measuring 6cm in length and 1.5cm deep. It was a gaping slash with an irregular shape.

Johnson took two and a half hours to complete Donald's post-mortem. He took blood samples, a mouth swab, a strand of hair and a urine sample for later forensic examination. He determined that Donald had died from multiple incised wounds, the most relevant to his death being the stab wound to the heart and the slicing of the jugular vein in his neck. The cuts to Donald's hands were especially worrying. They could well be defence wounds from an attacker wielding a knife. Another possibility was that Donald had cut himself picking up a sharp shard of the ceramic hot-water bottle found smashed to pieces in the bedroom.

At 6 a.m. the same morning, Johnson began work on Auriel's autopsy. Time was of the essence. If there was a killer on the loose in Cheshire, it would mean a full manhunt, and the police would need every clue they could glean from the victims' bodies. There was likely to be considerable attention from the press: a double murder in Wilmslow was big news, and for police inquiries media scrutiny comes with its own unique pressures. The spotlight would fall keenly upon whoever was made the senior investigating officer, or SIO in police slang. The police officers at the hospital wondered what sort of person could be capable of such a murder. A psychotic? A sadist? An individual with a history of mental illness?

Auriel had a number of wounds on her upper neck, where she had been stabbed repeatedly with a sharp object. One of those wounds had cut her carotid artery, one of the major blood vessels which supply blood to the brain, neck and face. On the left side of her neck were more stab wounds, which had severed her jugular vein. Across her forehead and on the side of her head were lacerations which split the skin. She had wounds on the left side of her chest. Bruises on her right leg. Bruises on her right arm. On her thigh. She had marks on her wrists and hands.

Had there been a sexual assault? Johnson told the officers he could not be certain. But what he did determine was that Auriel had died as a result of a sustained assault during which she received numerous impact injuries to her head from a blunt object. At some point during the attack she was throttled. She was stabbed in the neck up to a dozen times. It was not possible to say the order in which those events had occurred. He could not rule out some of the injuries being inflicted after she died.

Auriel's killer had shown no mercy. The number of injuries she had sustained was far in excess of what would have been required to kill her. Crime scene analysts who would examine the evidence a few days later would describe Auriel's injuries as 'expressive', which meant the violence went far beyond the mere functionality of trying to kill. This was an act of hatred, either for Auriel herself or perhaps the type of person she represented: a wealthy and middle-class woman living a life of comfort and contentment.

Walking bleary-eyed from the mortuary of Macclesfield General Hospital into the morning sunlight, Detective Superintendent Hood knew a decision had to be made quickly about who should lead the investigation. Hood would assume ultimate oversight, but he would need a man on the ground to lead the team and manage the day-to-day work of a major murder inquiry. Wilmslow had its own CID team, but the highest rank at the station was detective inspector. This job was high-profile. Hood felt it would need somebody of more senior rank.

Detective Chief Inspector John Davis was in charge of Macclesfield CID, the divisional headquarters which covered the Wilmslow area. Tall, dark-haired with a shrub of a moustache, Davis was an intelligent and well-spoken man, known for his love of the *Guardian* crossword and, given the right mood, a cigar. Here, Hood felt, was the man for the job. By 9 a.m. on Saturday morning, Davis was appointed the SIO, with Acting Detective Inspector Pearson as his deputy. Detective Constable Beale was appointed as family liaison officer (FLO), to deal directly with the three sons and their respective families.

The investigation was given a home at the major incident room in Macclesfield Police Station. It would also be supported by HOLMES II, short for the Home Office Large Major Enquiry System, the computer system that had been one product of the disastrous investigation into the Yorkshire Ripper, which had been entirely carried out on paper. Thirty thousand witness statements. A quarter of a million names. Millions of car number plates. But not a single computer. There had been so many boxes of evidence, in the form of handwritten index cards, that the floor of the incident room at Leeds' Millgarth Police Station had had to be reinforced to bear the weight.

Peter Sutcliffe had been interviewed nine times but he still wasn't caught. It was pure fluke that two patrol officers had stumbled upon his car one night in the red-light district of Sheffield, where he was found with 24-year-old prostitute Olivia Reivers, and discovered that the car had false number plates. The rest is history. But a report by Sir Lawrence Byford, the Inspector of Constabulary, found the ineffectiveness of the incident room had been a major handicap to the Ripper investigation. 'The backlog of unprocessed information,' said

Byford, 'resulted in the failure to connect vital pieces of related information.'

From the ashes of that inquiry came HOLMES, which for the first time allowed information to be stored and indexed on computers, with a facility for cross-referencing. SIOs would no longer be required to carry every detail of a case in their heads, which on complex homicide investigations was impossible anyway. By the '90s the Victorian notion of detective work as an art form was evolving into the scientific approach pioneered in the United States by the FBI, but it wasn't there yet. It would take the murder of a young black man by a group of racist thugs in south-east London, and a series of damning reports into the Met's failings, for detective work to fully begin to modernise at the turn of the twenty-first century.

DCI Davis would have HOLMES at his disposal and a team of detectives to deploy on the ground. He believed Donald and Auriel had been murdered in their own home, in a crime which was causing considerable anxiety in Wilmslow. There is nothing more terrifying in the mind of the public than the thought of a psychopath who is prepared to enter your own home in order to carry out an apparently motiveless murder. The hunt was on to catch the killer. They called it *Operation Menu*.

7

The Backdoor Murders

It was Monday, two days after the Wards were found dead, and the police were setting up roadblocks across Wilmslow to stop and question drivers and pedestrians. DCI Davis hoped it might help jog people's memories. They might just get lucky. A member of the public might have seen somebody acting suspicious around Lacey Grove. Davis wanted as many people as possible to come forward and provide any information they had about the Wards. He appealed to Wilmslow's residents to check their gardens for any bloody clothes that might have been dumped by the killer, or killers. Davis hadn't completely ruled out the idea that they could be looking at more than one person being involved. The newspapers and TV stations were full of news about the murders.

'COUPLE FOUND STABBED TO DEATH IN BED — MURDER', said *The Times*, in an article written by the newspaper's legendary northern correspondent Russell Jenkins. 'POLICE EXAMINING WEAPON USED TO KILL RETIRED COUPLE — KNIFE CLUE TO DOUBLE MURDER', said the *Manchester Evening News*. The *Daily Mail* called it the 'back door murder'. 'HOW SECURITY CONSCIOUS COUPLE WERE STABBED BY WALK-IN KILLER', the newspaper said.

Neighbours, including Francis Lee, the former owner of

Manchester City, who lived just up the road, were besieged by police officers and reporters. 'How anyone could brutally murder an elderly man and his own wife in their bed beggars belief,' a local woman told the papers. The *Daily Mail* report revealed a spate of recent burglaries in the neighbourhood. 'One night last week they left their back door unlocked by mistake,' the article said. 'That was the night an intruder walked in and stabbed them both to death as they prepared for bed.' David Kenyon, a neighbour of the Wards, was quoted in the same article saying there had been 'lots of robberies' in the area. 'This part of Wilmslow has been hit particularly hard,' he said. 'But you still don't expect this sort of violence.' The reporters were briefed by senior detectives that the couple had 'fought for their lives' during the attack.

'They were obviously very security-conscious,' said Davis,

but it appears that on the night they were killed the back door had been left unlocked. They were subjected to a sustained attack and both had multiple knife wounds. At the moment we have not established a motive for this terrible crime, but we have not ruled out robbery. We won't know if anything has been taken until we are in a position to let family members into the house. However, I can confirm that the Wards' car is still in the garage. The attacker would have been heavily bloodstained, and we are appealing to anyone who saw anything suspicious in and around the area last Monday to contact us immediately.

Cheshire Police said there were 'clear signs' that Donald had struggled with the attacker. This was following an examination of the Wards' bedroom by detectives, SOCOs and the pathologist, interviews with family members and post-mortem examinations of both bodies by the pathologist. 'Post-mortem examinations revealed they had been victims of a vicious attack,' Davis told the press. 'There is nothing to indicate that they were anything other than a happy couple.'

SOCOs and forensic scientists from the Cheshire Constabulary Scientific Support Unit had set up camp in a marquee outside the Wards' home. A second marquee was erected next door in front of Wendy Smith's house. Initially Wendy was quite alarmed at the thought of a major manhunt being conducted from her driveway, but at least she was in a street full of police officers, which probably made her house the safest place to be in the county. Droves of police officers popped in and out of her house to use the loo, while her two children were put to good use making them cups of tea. Police found a pair of hospital-type gloves in the Wards' bins and Wendy, being a hospital nurse, was questioned about it. They were the same gloves she had used while dressing Donald's cut from the broken light bulb. They quickly ruled her out of their enquiries.

On Tuesday, the Ward family broke their silence. Simon, David and Michael released a joint statement to the public. 'We are all deeply shocked by the loss of our parents who died in such tragic circumstances,' read the statement.

> They were kind, caring and helpful to everyone. They were close to us as parents and grandparents. They were especially devoted to children – be they grandchildren, nephews and nieces or great nephews and nieces. They showed their devotion by making time for everyone with their generosity of

spirit. They kept active contact with a wide range of friends and relatives of all ages across the country and around the world. They will be greatly missed.

The police focused their enquiries on house-to-house canvassing, media appeals and interviews with family and friends, as they tried to establish the Wards' movements for the two weeks leading up to their deaths. The priority was pinning down exactly when they had died. This would help Operation Menu focus on a specific timeframe and allow possible suspects to be ruled in or out of the investigation.

Davis reasoned that Donald and Auriel were most likely to have died shortly after 6.30 a.m. on Tuesday, 23 November. There were a number of clues which had enabled him to arrive at this conclusion. The telephone company had provided the inquiry team with a list of outgoing and incoming calls for the property. There were no outgoing calls from Monday evening, and nothing incoming was answered, either. Medicines in the house had been taken up until Monday. There were no entries in the Wards' diary after Monday. Their diary on most days had a line or two noting appointments, meetings with friends or observations about the day.

The service engineers at ADT, the alarm company contracted by the Wards to provide their security, said the house alarm was switched off at precisely 6.29 a.m. on Tuesday morning using the correct code. The newspapers delivered after Monday had been found by the front door, undisturbed, lying in chronological order. Dr Johnson, the Home Office pathologist, also concurred that the decomposition of the two bodies was consistent with death after three to four days. Either the killer had been allowed inside the house, detectives thought, or he had pushed his way inside, or had a key which he used after 6.30 a.m. when the alarm was deactivated.

More often than not in murder cases, the assailant is known to their victim, and family members are typically among the first people who have to be examined and ruled out of any inquiry. The couple had left a sizeable estate: £700,000 in today's money. Michael, David and Simon fully assisted the police investigation, and their movements and financial backgrounds were examined at length. There was nothing to suggest any motive or culpability for their parents' murder, and they were eliminated from enquiries.

James Allen was considered. He was resurfacing the Wards' driveway at the time. He was also one of the last people to see them alive. The police searched his house and his van, and at one point Allen even thought he was being followed by undercover officers. He was grilled by detectives, who wanted to know every detail about his contact with Donald and Auriel in the days leading up to their deaths. One of the officers told him it was 'just procedure': they wanted to rule him out of their inquiries. Allen told him that was fine, but once it was over and he was ruled out, he wanted an apology. He never got one.

There was no suggestion that Allen had anything to do with the murders, and he became an important witness for Operation Menu. He told police the Wards had seemed happy and content when he last saw them on the Monday. He repeated what family members had already told the police about Donald being careful with house security. It wasn't like him to leave a door unlocked. The whole experience was a difficult time for Allen, and not a time in his life he liked to dwell on. But his time being interrogated would leave him with a strange sense of reassurance that if any of his loved ones were ever killed in such circumstances, Cheshire Police would do everything in its power to identify the person responsible.

Davis had deployed officers on the ground in Wilmslow to canvas neighbours, residents, motorists and anybody else who might have seen anything on Monday evening or Tuesday morning. And he got a breakthrough. Several leads came in of people acting suspiciously. Davis ordered the descriptions and computer E-fits of two men they wanted to identify to be issued to the media. At 9.30 a.m. on Tuesday, 23 November, a white man had been seen approaching Tatton Court flats in Handforth, from the direction of Tatton Road, less than two miles from the Wards' home. He pressed buttons on the intercom panel to gain entry. He had blood on his hands. He was five feet nine inches in height, thirty-five to thirty-eight years old, with short dark hair receding in the middle and at the front. He was stockily built, with a tooth missing. He wore a khaki-green canvas jacket with a fur-trimmed hood and a pair of dark-blue trousers.

At 9.20 p.m. the same day, a second man was spotted in Lacey Green staring at passers-by in a suspicious manner. This person was said by witnesses to be slim and white, aged thirty, about five feet five inches tall, with a lean, high-cheek-boned face. He was said to have worn a blue-black, snug-fitting woollen hat pulled down almost to his eyebrows, a purple, shiny bubble jacket and a pair of faded denim jeans, with dark-coloured shoes or trainers.

In the days after publishing the E-fits of the two suspects, officers received more than thirty calls from members of the public. Of particular interest to the inquiry team was the man trying to get inside Tatton Court flats the very morning the Wards were killed. It fitted both the time and the geography of the murders. Who was he? And why did he have blood on his hands? Operation Menu was under pressure from the top brass and the public. It needed answers.

On a cold afternoon in November, Christine Hurst turned up at Macclesfield Hospital's mortuary to go through the death reports that had come in overnight. The year before, she had been promoted to senior coroner's officer for Cheshire, and now led a sizeable team working across the four areas of the county, comprising Warrington, Macclesfield, Chester and Crewe. Her busy job had just got busier. She still investigated cases, but now had oversight for cases being examined by her team of coroner's officers.

Dave Bourne, one of the hospital's long-standing mortuary technicians, opened up one of the fridge doors and drew out one of the stacks of tiers where the bodies lay. Hurst was carrying out what was known as an 'identification confirmation' on a person who had died on a ward in Macclesfield Hospital over the weekend, gathering the person's medical information on behalf of the coroner. She checked the person's hospital wristband, which carried the patient's name, date of birth and patient number, so the coroner's office could be certain of a person's identity before a post-mortem examination was ordered.

Hurst saw there was no need to get the family to do an identification. The hospital's records were all in order. Bourne ran a tight ship. The mortuary was always immaculately clean.

There were no smells of decomposing bodies, unlike some of the other mortuaries in the region, where the whiff of a corpse in the air was not uncommon. At Bourne's mortuary relatives who wanted to view their loved ones for one final time were always treated with the upmost respect. Bourne and Hurst shared the same approach to death. Hurst had seen plenty of 'dark, cop humour' at Macclesfield Police Station during her time. People could become quite cynical about dead bodies. That wasn't for her. She had never found that sort of black humour funny. She always put herself in the family's position. She would think about her mother, or her sister – she knew how it felt to lose a loved one. The thought of somebody inappropriately joking behind the scenes was not something she wanted to be a part of.

They were about to finish up the ID when Hurst glanced down at the body underneath, lying on a tray on the bottom tier. It was Auriel Ward. Hurst saw her head injuries. Her mouth dropped open and her heart started racing. She couldn't believe what she was seeing. Those wounds. The blunt-force trauma combined with the use of a sharp implement. The extreme violence. It was history repeating itself. Hurst saw that Auriel's hair had been washed – a tell-tale sign that the post-mortem had already taken place.

'What's this case?' she asked Bourne. It was clearly not a natural death, and would be destined for the attentions of the coroner. It would be useful to get an early heads-up about the circumstances of the lady's death before the report landed in the office.

'Husband and wife killed over the weekend. Found dead in the bedroom of their house.'

'Where did they live?'

'Wilmslow.'

'You're *kidding* . . .'

Bourne wasn't kidding. Like Hurst, he never joked about such matters. Hurst returned to her office at Macclesfield Police Station. She couldn't get the sight of Auriel Ward out of her head. Her injuries were so similar to Bea Ainsworth's. Several days later she received the crime scene photographs from the SOCOs. She saw the Wards' bodies lying in their blood-soaked bed. Donald on the left. Auriel on the right. Auriel with a pillow over her head, her nightdress hitched up to reveal her pubic area.

She had seen it all before three years ago. She needed to find out more. Hurst was cautious by her nature. She was a rational creature and rarely acted on impulse. She was concerned she would appear fanciful and melodramatic if she started openly claiming the two Wilmslow cases might be linked. She had to be clever about it. She was friendly with one of the SOCOs, a woman who Hurst managed to bump into one day by the photocopiers in the corridor outside their respective offices in the station.

'Hiya, Christine. How was your holiday?'

'Good, thanks. Are you on the Wards' case?'

'Yes. Awful.'

'I know. Look, have you got a minute? There's something I'd like you to see.'

The SOCO waited while Hurst went into her office and took out the coroner's file on the Ainsworths. She kept all her files in the office for three years before sending them off to the archives in the basement of Warrington Town Hall, a veritable library of death, recording all the strange, unexpected and unnatural deaths which had occurred in the county.

'Ever heard of Howard and Bea Ainsworth?' Hurst asked her.

The SOCO shook her head.

'It was a murder-suicide in 1996 in Wilmslow. The police said Howard murdered his wife and then killed himself. I never believed it. I always wondered if somebody else killed them. When I saw Auriel in the mortuary, her injuries looked almost identical to Bea Ainsworth's injuries. That's a big coincidence, don't you think?'

The SOCO examined the photographs. She frowned.

'What?' Hurst asked, seeing her reaction.

'I think there was a pillow left on Auriel's face, too,' said the SOCO.

'Just like Bea Ainsworth?'

She nodded. 'And the position of the nightie is the same,' the SOCO admitted. 'You're right. There are similar, aren't they?'

Hurst had satisfied herself. She wasn't going mad. She decided to raise the links with two separate police officers. The Ainsworths' case was being overlooked, probably because of the original determination of murder-suicide, which for Hurst had failed to take into account some of the inconsistencies in the evidence.

She explained the parallels between the Ainsworths and the Wards. Wasn't it an incredible coincidence that the nightdresses of both women had been yanked up to expose them?

Hurst was brushed off. It's all in hand. Don't worry about it. Must get on. Thanks for raising it. Hurst felt her chest swell with frustration. Three years and one promotion later, she still wasn't being taken seriously. It was the same old story. What did she know? How could they have missed something that was being pointed out to them by a civilian investigator from the coroner's office?

By mid-December, Operation Menu was struggling to identify a credible suspect for a double murder. The E-fit leads had come to nothing. The forensic investigations had failed to identify a third party in the house. There were no eyewitnesses. No CCTV. Davis had already begun to hypothesise around the negative results. That's the way police investigations can work, sometimes. After all, what is not found at the crime scene can often be just as important to a detective as what is found. They hadn't identified another person's DNA or fingerprints in the house, and at some point a line had to be drawn in terms of budget and resources. They could only look for so long. A complex murder inquiry didn't mean the rest of the bodies stopped stacking up in Cheshire overnight. The backlog was building. Soon enough, the top brass would want their manpower back from Operation Menu. The lack of third-party evidence in the house meant some members of the inquiry team began to suspect the unthinkable. Perhaps it wasn't a rogue intruder who had broken into the house to slaughter the Wards after all. Maybe the murderer was Donald?

8

Occam's Razor

Any detective worth his salt will say that most murder inquiries have a prime suspect inside the first twenty-four to forty-eight hours. It is the key window for any murder inquiry, known as the 'golden hours'. Most police investigations are either blown or placed on a firm footing during that time period. Crime scenes should be sealed off for forensic analysis. Any relevant witnesses should be interviewed on the spot, before stories can be devised and alibis arranged. And proper records of those interviews should be kept for future consideration. If you don't have a suspect inside that time frame, then you could be looking at a dreaded whodunnit. It was December now, and Operation Menu still had no solid third-party suspect. The leads and tip-offs on possible sightings had dwindled away to nothing. The team began to look more carefully at Donald and Auriel Ward.

They had no criminal convictions, and had never been known to the police or social services in any way. There was no history of domestic violence between the couple, and not a shred of evidence to suggest Donald had laid a finger in anger upon his wife during forty-five years of marriage. Quite the opposite. They were besotted with one another and enjoyed the sort of marriage that most would envy.

Davis's team looked into Donald's medical history hoping it might reveal some clues. Mary Vipond, who had known the couple for three decades, told the police that Auriel was worried about Donald's recent weight loss. Donald weighed just over ten stone and Auriel wanted to fatten him up. Ever since his heart attack Donald had had a 'thing' about keeping trim. Auriel suspected that he was secretly disposing of his food. If he was, it did not appear to be a serious problem. His post-mortem examination made reference to the fact that he was 'well nourished'.

Donald kept a 'watching brief' on his health, according to his doctor. Like the Ainsworths, the Wards used the Kenmore Medical Centre. His most serious illness was the heart attack in September 1987. He contracted bronchitis in 1991. Then four years later he went through a cancer scare, which turned out to be an ulcer. In January 1996, he underwent a colonoscopy in search for polyps – abnormal tissue growths that can look like small flat bumps or tiny mushroom-like stalks and have the potential to turn into cancer. No polyps were found. Following his heart attack Donald had regular check-ups on his cholesterol level. Nothing especially unusual about that. Many elderly people start to think more about their health as they get older, taking care of themselves as best they can in order to get the most out of the rest of their lives. Donald was no different. He was keen on getting check-ups. 'Better safe than sorry' was Donald's motto when it came to his health. He was placed on atorvastatin, a drug which can help lower cholesterol levels. He was still taking atorvastatin when he died.

During Donald's last visit to his doctor, he complained of prostate trouble. Donald was more than aware that prostate problems can turn cancerous. A blood test was carried out on 19 November 1999. The result, which was negative, was not known until after his death. Donald and Auriel's diary, found in their house at Lacey Grove, contained an entry for that appointment. *Donald, Dr 10.35 a.m.* Four days earlier another entry had been written. *Donald suffering water problems. Stress.* The word stress was underlined. The police considered this key evidence pointing towards the conclusion that Donald had killed his wife. Donald's stress about his cancer test, they proposed, may have served as a trigger for the murder, followed by his own suicide. It was the best the inquiry team could come up with in terms of a rationale for the killings. Except that, apart from the false cancer alarm, Donald was in good health.

The medical records show that Auriel was also in relatively good condition for her age. Her GP at the Kenmore practice, Dr Case, told the police that she had no significant illnesses, apart from two hip replacements. Her sons suspected she suffered from aches in her hips from time to time, but she was never known to complain openly to anybody about the pain. She was found to be blind in her left eye and was on medication for back problems. She had a history of arthritis. But like Donald she had no major health concerns.

The police began to connect certain events leading up to their deaths which they believed to be odd or out of character. After the birthday meal at the Bridge Hotel in Prestbury with Simon, detectives discovered, the Wards had updated their wills with the current addresses of their children. The paperwork was recovered from the house. What might that suggest? A suicide pact? That Donald was plotting to murder Auriel? A few hours earlier he had been blowing out the candles on his wife's birthday cake, and a few days before that, wrapping his coat around her shoulders to stop her getting wet in the rain. DCI Davis believed the updating of the wills may have been part of a 'settling of affairs' by Donald, who was known to be quite particular. He certainly wasn't the sort of person who would want to leave any loose ends in the event of his death. He would want everything to be neat and tidy.

Susan Nobes, the manager at his newsagent's on Dean Row Road, told the police that he paid his newspaper bill for five days in advance, rather than the usual two days. The police again viewed this as Donald settling his affairs before the murder. But logic begs the question: if Donald was planning to murder his wife and kill himself on Tuesday, why would he still want the papers to be delivered on Wednesday, Thursday and Friday?

The last known person to speak to Donald was James Allen, the handyman. Allen had called him at 5 p.m. to confirm that he owed £785 for the driveway, and then received the cheque and a thank-you note in the post the next day. An entry in the Wards' diary on Monday read: *Donald posted chq.* This was also considered by the police to be another sign of Donald tying up his business affairs.

From Monday evening, the events inside the house start to get a little hazy. The police had to rely upon a jigsaw of evidence gleaned from forensic examination, post-mortem examination and crime scene specialists, who tried to piece together what they thought was the most likely narrative to explain what had happened. After all, there were no eyewitnesses. No CCTV. The police were left with informed guesswork based on the available facts.

At the request of the inquiry team, a service engineer

employed by ADT Alarms, Paul Birch, examined the alarm system at the Wards' bungalow. He found the alarm was set at 10.20 p.m. on Monday. It was switched off at precisely 6.29 a.m. on Tuesday. The police assumed the Wards were still alive during that window. The next time a code was entered into the alarm system was on Friday, when Roger Bugler, their neighbour, typed in the correct access code just before 5 p.m., thinking that he would have to disable the alarm to prevent it from activating while he and Stanley Martlew carried out their search of the house.

The police asked ADT to chart fourteen days of usage – from 12 to 25 November. It showed a regular pattern. The Wards would set their alarm at 10.30 p.m. each evening, then switch it off at 6.30 a.m. the next morning. There was a slight inconsistency when the alarm was not set for 28 hours between 10.04 a.m. on 13 November and 2.02 p.m. on 14 November. After that, the alarm was then set and switched off several times over the next two days. The reasons for this remain unknown. In addition, the two downstairs bedrooms had independent alarms which activated when police officers searching the house entered the bedrooms. The Wards had a table lamp in a front room of the house set up to switch on and off three times a day using an automatic timer, and the curtains opened and closed by use of another timer.

There were several unconfirmed sightings of Donald after Tuesday by David Sydenham, the paper boy, as well as Wendy and her daughter Laura. Sydenham says he saw Donald on the Tuesday, Wednesday and Thursday. He thought he actually gave Donald his newspaper on Tuesday by placing it in his hand. But the newspaper was found behind the front door, beneath the letter box. Fingerprint tests were conducted to check if Donald or Auriel had handled any of the papers. The results came back negative.

Wendy's daughter thought she saw the lights on in the Wards' house and Donald at the kitchen window at just before 5 p.m. on Wednesday. Wendy also thought she might have seen Donald on Thursday when she was talking to James Allen. The sighting was not confirmed by Allen. All those sightings were discounted by the police. This was not unusual in itself. Any complex murder inquiry will usually feature some conflicting witness testimony. It was the job of the lead detective, DCI Davis, to sift through that evidence to work out what should be ruled in or out of the inquiry's timeline.

The forensic teams looked for any sign that a third party had entered the house and murdered the Wards. None could be found. As a result, the inquiry team began to draw conclusions from the negatives. No glove marks could be found in the house, which might suggest that if there was an offender who entered the property, there should be clusters of fingerprints in the Wards' bedroom. The lack of fingerprint clusters steered the police towards believing that nobody else was inside the house. However, this was not the same as being able to rule out an intruder entirely. Far from it.

One of Scotland Yard's most senior detectives, Hamish Campbell, who was in charge of the investigation into the MI6 spy Gareth Williams, the so-called 'Spy in the Bag' case, once warned of the dangers of reading a negative as conclusive proof. Williams was found dead in a red holdall padlocked on the outside with the keys found inside. It was a truly baffling case. The conundrum for detectives was whether Williams had locked himself inside the bag alone, or if somebody was with him at the time, who perhaps had walked out and left him to die, making it murder.

Jackie Sebire, the detective chief inspector on that case, told the inquest hearing that the fact Williams had left no fingerprints on the bathroom tiles or bathtub made it more likely he was with another person. Otherwise, she said, she would have expected to see his fingerprints on the walls of the shower. The absence of them suggested to her that he had help getting into the holdall. Campbell would later question this logic. 'My issue with that is: where is the evidence base?' said Campbell.

Who is to say a person has to leave fingerprints on their bathroom tiles when getting into a bag in such a way? We have this idea that people leave fingerprints everywhere. I once investigated the murder of a man inside his own home. When we did the forensics, we couldn't find a single fingerprint belonging to the victim. Not one. You might think – well – how is that possible? Well, it just is. The absence of evidence is not an absolute proof in itself.

The toxicology results threw up very little useful information for Operation Menu. There were no indications that Donald and Auriel had been affected by drink or drugs at the time of the incident. Donald was found to have paracetamol in his bloodstream consistent with a normal dosage. The drug would not be expected to affect a person's mood or behaviour.

One of the most influential reports received by the police was carried out by the Forensic Science Service (FSS). Two forensic science officers, one of them the experienced forensic scientist Sarah Brownhill, visited the Wards' home the day after their bodies were discovered. By the time Brownhill arrived at the house, Donald and Auriel's bodies had been transported to the mortuary, and some of the bedding in the main bedroom had also been removed.

Brownhill's task, along with her colleague Mr Hignett, was to examine the bloodstaining in the house. Their focus would be the main bedroom, the hallway and stairs, and the kitchen. One of the first things Brownhill noticed were the heavily bloodstained pillows on the bed and the head end of the bottom sheet. Some of the blood on the sheet appeared diffuse — as if it was somehow diluted.

Towards the end of the bed, Brownhill noticed an area of congealed blood. The sheet and the board at the foot of the bed were smeared with blood. The headboard and wall above the headboard were spattered with spots of blood. Again, some of the spots looked diluted. On the bedside cabinet on Auriel's side, a Teasmade — a machine for making tea automatically — had spots of blood on the casing. There was also blood on the lead going into the plug socket. Next to the Teasmade was the telephone, which was connected to the wall. The phone had blood on the plug socket and the telephone cable.

Brownhill left the bedroom and started to work along the upstairs landing to the staircase, following the trail. She noticed blood on the banisters and drops of blood on the stairs. A loose flake of blood was present on the carpet on the middle landing. Bloody fingerprints were on the edge of the windowsill. A droplet of blood was on the carpet at the bottom of the stairs, and another on the carpet just inside the dining room.

She was at the foot of the stairs now, in the hallway. From there, a door led into the dining room. The door handle on the hall side of this door was smeared with blood, and there was blood on the surface of the door, the edge of the door and the door jamb on the unhinged side. She followed the trail of blood to the kitchen. On the left-hand wall of the kitchen as you enter from the dining room was a light switch. The switch had smears of blood on it, as did the edge of the door frame close to the light switch.

In the kitchen sink there was a washing-up bowl containing a dry dishcloth, which was bloodstained. A heavy-contact blood-stain was present on the outer surface of a drawer just to the right of the sink. This was a cutlery drawer containing knives. The top part of this staining appeared dilute. There were no bloodstains or blood droplets inside the drawer. Brownhill found bloodstaining on a second drawer next to the fridge. Blood was visible inside this drawer; blood droplets had been dripped onto a tea towel and a set of keys. Another set of keys on a keyring were found in a lock on the inside of the kitchen door. They were bloodstained, as was the door handle on the inside of the kitchen door.

The forensic scientists took swabs of their findings around the house. Their search complete, they returned to the labo-ratory, where they used biological material from Donald and Auriel to build a DNA profile. The profile would then be used as a reference point to test against the bloodstains found around the house and build up a picture of their movements. Between 29 November and 15 December, a total of sixty-seven items were submitted by police to Brownhill's FSS laboratory in Chorley. These items were the blood samples taken from the blood trail around the house, the weapons, the Wards' nightclothes and their bloodstained bedding.

The forensic report the two scientists eventually produced would begin to change the narrative in favour of Donald being the killer. The scientists found that Auriel was clutching a number of hairs, probably as a result of her reaching her right hand up to one of her cuts. Donald had Auriel's blood on his right foot and right knee.

The kitchen knife found in Donald's chest, puncturing his heart, measured 23cm and featured a single serrated cutting edge. Blood on the tip and handle of the knife belonged to Donald. Blood on the end of the blade, and on the hilt, belonged to Donald and Auriel. The blood on the telephone cable was Donald's. The laboratory was unable to achieve a match for Donald or Auriel on the two bloodstained handkerchiefs found in the bedroom. The DNA had degraded too much for a precise match. A blood-grouping test showed that one of the handkerchiefs had stains with the same blood types as Donald and Auriel, while the second handkerchief had the same blood type as Donald's blood.

The forensic results around the smashed ceramic hot-water bottle were one of the most important clues left behind for the investigation team. It was also the evidence which the police believed implicated Donald. The ceramic pot was broken into several large fragments with sharp edges. The fragments contained a mixture of Donald and Auriel's blood. One of those fragments, roughly triangular in shape, had bloodstaining on the inner and outer surfaces and on the broken edges. At the point of the 'triangle' was some fatty tissue. Fragments of hair, too. The DNA profiles obtained from this piece showed a mixture of Donald's and Auriel's blood.

Moving to the findings in the kitchen, the blood on three keys on the ring found in the kitchen door was Donald's. Brownhill also found Donald's blood in the passageway outside the kitchen door. A flake of blood found on the kitchen cutlery drawer close to the sink was Donald's, as was the blood on the outside of the drawer. There was blood on a dishcloth in a bowl – but no DNA profile could be extracted. A single light switch in the kitchen was also smeared with blood from Donald and Auriel.

As with any forensic analysis, the bloodstains were like pieces of a jigsaw which, pieced together in a certain way, could create a certain picture. Pieced together another way, the picture could look entirely different. The FSS report came up with a conclusion which it said could 'realistically account' for the Wards' deaths. The account was as follows.

Auriel was attacked in the bed in the spot where she was subsequently found. Donald probably carried out the attack using the ceramic hot-water bottle, possibly by slamming the heavy bottle down on Auriel's head. The ceramic bottle broke into several fragments, causing the water inside to wet the bedclothes, Donald's pyjamas and Auriel's nightgown, which would explain the diffuse bloodstaining. Donald used the broken pieces to stab his wife, but while doing so cut his hand, which could explain the deep slice on his palm, along with the presence of his and his wife's blood on the broken pieces of the pot.

After Donald hurt his hand, he partially, but not fully,

removed the telephone cable from its socket, transferring his blood to the socket, the cable, the connector and the Teasmade lead. He then went downstairs, dripping blood onto the carpet, smearing blood along the banister. He stumbled through the door into the dining room, leaving blood on the door handle, and entered the kitchen. He flicked on the light, depositing his and his wife's blood onto the switch. There was no way of knowing the order of events which happened next, but at some point Donald had apparently tried to stem his blood using the dishcloth in the washing-up bowl.

He opened a drawer on the opposite side of the kitchen and, for reasons which remain a mystery, took the back-door keys from the pot in the key drawer and inserted the bloodstained keys into the lock on the inside of the kitchen door. He opened the door and dripped some blood onto a seed tray in the passageway just outside the kitchen and transferred blood to the light switch in the passageway.

Donald then went back inside the house and didn't lock the door. He opened the drawer to the right of the sink and took out a knife, possibly two knives. He transferred blood from his bleeding hand to the outside of the drawer, but avoided dripping any blood into the inside of the cutlery drawer while taking out the knives. He went upstairs, got into bed beside his murdered wife, whom he had apparently tucked in with a fluffy pink blanket, and sliced his throat, creating a wound almost the width of his neck. His neck spurting with blood, he then took up the same knife and plunged the blade directly into his heart, ending his life.

The extraordinary account of violence inflicted by Donald upon his wife and himself began to sway DCI Davis and his team. Davis relied heavily upon the narrative summary of events in the FSS report for his own summary report for the coroner, which provided Operation Menu's homework and conclusions about the Wards' deaths. But there were problems with this version of events. It conflicted with the findings of another set of police experts, who had found evidence that Donald's body had been moved after his death. These additional investigators also questioned if it was physically possible to cut your throat and jugular vein and still be able to stab yourself directly in the heart. Some were far from convinced.

Every detective in the UK, either knowingly or unknowingly, has been trained to build a case based upon the principles of Occam's Razor, a principle of philosophy developed by William of Occam, a fourteenth-century Franciscan friar. Occam's theory was simply this: suppose there exist two different explanations for a single occurrence. In this situation, the explanation which requires the smallest number of assumptions is usually the correct one. This is another way of saying that the more assumptions you have to make, the more unlikely an explanation will be. Detectives are trained to believe that the simplest explanation is most often the right one. Often. But not always.

There are many misconceptions about the role carried out by the coroner. Some people think it is their job to carry out post-mortem examinations or attend crime scenes. They imagine coroners to work like Quincy, in the US drama series starring Jack Klugman as a county medical examiner who would investigate what appeared to be normal deaths for clues that they might in fact be murder. The reality is very different.

It is acknowledged by parliament and society in general that investigating sudden, unnatural or unexplained deaths is in the best interests of the community. The role of the coroner has adapted over the past eight centuries since it was first established, in 1194, as a form of medieval tax gatherer. Gradually it evolved into being an independent judicial officer charged with the investigation of unexplained death.

According to the Coroners' Society, the duties of the early coroners could mean the investigation of almost any aspect of medieval life that had the potential benefit of revenue for the Crown. People who committed suicide, or *felo de se*, would have their estates made forfeit to the crown, as were shipwrecks, fires and any discovery of buried treasure in the community. After the Norman Conquest, in order to prevent Normans living in communities across England from being murdered, a heavy fine was levied on any village where a dead body was discovered, with the presumption that the dead person was Norman unless they could be proved to be English. The fine was known as the *murdrum*, from which the word 'murder' is derived. Early inquests would deal with the 'presumption of Normanry'. To avoid the fine, it would be the task of the local community to present a case that the dead person was in fact English.

The coroner system continued to adapt and grow over the centuries, until the nineteenth century, when major reform was brought to the investigation of death in the community. In 1836, the Births and Deaths Registration Act was passed, prompted by the inaccurate recording of deaths arising from epidemics such as cholera. There was also a growing political and public concern that easy access to uncontrolled poisons, and an inadequate medical investigation into the causes of death, was allowing many homicides to go undetected. By the late nineteenth century the coroner's fiscal responsibilities had begun to disappear, as coroners became more concerned with establishing the circumstances of violent and unnatural deaths for the benefit of the community.

Today, the coroner service will investigate over one third of all deaths in England and Wales. Coroners will often have substantial experience working as a lawyer or a medical doctor. They are appointed to work in set geographical areas, and each area has a certain number of coroners, depending on its size and population. The coroner's investigators, known as coroner's officers, will then inquire about a death once a report is received about a body within the jurisdiction.

In December 1999, the chief coroner for Cheshire, Nicholas Rheinberg, asked for a second post-mortem to be carried out on the bodies of Donald and Auriel Ward. Earlier in the year, Rheinberg had taken over the job of senior coroner in the county from John Hibbert. Where the veteran Hibbert, nicknamed the 'caring coroner', disliked putting the families through the coronial process, and would shield them from lengthy inquests, Rheinberg brought a different approach. A stickler for detail, he had learnt long ago to step back from the harsh realities of the job in order to help families find the answers they need to move on. Dealing with human misery on a daily basis was part of the job. Bringing public scrutiny to bear on the death of a loved one was a difficult process for lots of families, many of whom would like to get on with grieving, but Rheinberg had a belief that an inquest could help families achieve closure by providing them with a full and accurate account of a loved one's death.

The task of carrying out the second autopsy on the Wards fell to Dr Alan Williams, the Home Office pathologist who had examined the Ainsworths. Auriel was re-examined at 3 p.m. on 17 December in the mortuary of Macclesfield District General Hospital. Donald's post-mortem took place an hour later. The original pathologist, Dr Paul Johnson, was also present along with Superintendent Hood, two SOCOs and a handful of junior detectives.

The findings were similar to the first autopsies. Auriel died from strangulation and stab wounds to the neck. Williams was not able to determine if the strangulation had been carried out before or after she died. He believed that Donald's neck wound was typical of a self-inflicted wound. Williams found that the wounds on Auriel were likely to have been inflicted by Donald, who had subsequently died from self-inflicted injuries.

DCI Davis used the reports of the two pathologists and the forensic report to draw his conclusions. He believed the most likely explanation of Donald's wounded hand was that he had cut himself on a broken piece of pot while stabbing his wife with it. But the key in the kitchen door remained a mystery, as did the motive.

Why did Donald take the key out of the pot and put it in the lock? Why did he step outside then go back inside? One possible explanation, Davis thought, was that Donald had read about the murder-suicide case of the Ainsworths in the local news. Donald might have read that Howard had left the door open in order to facilitate access for loved ones. This, perhaps, was Donald being considerate for his sons – moments after stabbing their mother more than a dozen times in the neck.

In terms of a motive, Donald's stress because of his test

for prostate cancer might have tipped him over the edge into murder. It was thin, but it was all the investigation team had. The explanation made little sense to many of their loved ones. Donald had experienced cancer scares in the past. He had survived a heart attack. He was careful about his health. He wanted to prolong his life, not end it in such savagery. Some of his close family members were baffled by the idea that Donald would stab himself to death. Donald was a trained chemist. There were plenty of tablets in the house if he had wanted to take his own life. Why cut his throat and stab himself in the heart? On the surface, the police were heading towards a neat and tidy conclusion of the Wards' case. But then a report was submitted to the inquiry team by an elite unit of police investigators. And it pointed to evidence which might prove there had been another person in the house after all.

9

The Real Cracker

It was early December when two smartly dressed men walked
into the Wards' bungalow to inspect the scene and report back
their findings to DCI Davis. These were no ordinary detectives.
Detective Sergeant Simon Wells and Lee Rainbow, a senior
behavioural analyst, were part of the serious crime analysis unit
within the National Crime Faculty, or NCF, set up in 1997 by
the Home Office to provide the sort of expertise offered by the
FBI to law enforcement investigations in United States. The
NCF would write a report for Davis and its findings were kept
confidential. One of the NCF's requirements when it helped
Davis and his team was that the findings of its report could
never be disclosed to the accused as part of any future proceed-
ings. NCF crime scene reports were supposed to be treated as
intelligence, rather than evidence for court. The NCF at the
time knew that police forces were still uncertain about the
work of behavioural analysts and how their techniques could
help with major investigations. Such work was still considered
sensitive by the police, and reports involving the NCF were
marked for the lead detective's eyes only. The NCF considered
their reports a guide, to open up the mind to all the possibilities. Their experts were encouraged to think outside the box,

which required freedom to express their opinions, something which would be impossible in a formal statement.

Many of the functions of the NCF were eventually swallowed up by the College of Policing, but in 1999 it had a team of roughly thirty police officers, mostly on loan from other police forces. Its formation in the first place harked back to the Yorkshire Ripper case in the 1980s. A review of West Yorkshire Police's mammoth investigation by the Chief Inspector of Constabulary had found that detectives desperately needed more training to help them carry out complex investigations. But within policing at the time there was a deeper concern. Society was now throwing up random, opportunist killers whose crimes defied rational explanation. The traditional methods of detection, which had remained largely unchanged since the Victorian era, were struggling to catch serial offenders like the Yorkshire Ripper, whose crimes crossed the boundaries of different forces, causing confusion and delay in connecting the victims. Catching serial killers like Sutcliffe required a modern system of detective work which could link homicides and serious sex crimes to reveal patterns of behaviour.

Ever since Sherlock Holmes claimed that detective work should be approached as a science, the police have been trying to organise intuition into something more systematic. Chief police officers and senior detectives wanted a centre of excellence which could better define investigative strategies, give advice on complex cases and provide detectives with more training on advanced investigative techniques.

Part of the NCF's new role was to develop computer databases which could collate and analyse offence and offender characteristics from sexually motivated murders, child abductions and rape cases. The aim was to spot cases which might be linked together. This could mean looking into a string of similar rapes in a particular region of the country, or murders in different towns which crossed police force borders and came under separate forces but had comparable attributes, such as the method of attack or the type of victim being targeted.

The NCF would also develop expertise in offender profiling, a technique pioneered by the FBI since the mid-1970s, in an attempt to better understand the criminal mind. Offender profiling is a process which, in theory, allows investigators to draw conclusions about the perpetrator's identity from the traces found at the crime scene. Using the evidence left behind, there is an attempt to re-create the emotional and mental make-up of the criminal, their habits and domestic life, what sort of job they might do, where they might live. Even the way they might look.

When the NCF was brought into existence, the practice of offender profiling was regarded as controversial among many detectives in forces across the UK. Many viewed it simply as quackery and guesswork, a hopeless attempt to shortcut good policework. Most dangerous of all, some thought, was that offender profiling risked giving investigators tunnel vision. If presented with a 'profile' of the suspect which, for example, says that, based on that person's crimes, they should be hunting for a man in his early thirties who has recently divorced, plays rugby and may be a manual labourer, then there could be a risk that the investigators will only focus on finding and identifying people who fall within that category. At the time of writing, there are three or four 'investigative psychologists' currently being used by police forces in the UK. They do not like to use the term 'offender profilers' as this is only part of what they might do. They prefer to call themselves behavioural investigative advisers (BIAs).

The biggest blow to such techniques, which are more popular with law enforcement agencies in the United States, came during Scotland Yard's investigation into Colin Stagg, who was charged with the murder of Rachel Nickell on Wimbledon Common. In 1992 Rachel was walking with her two-year-old son Alex and her dog Molly when she was sexually assaulted and stabbed forty-nine times. Alex was found clinging to her blood-soaked body, begging, 'Get up, Mummy.' The public was outraged, and the pressure on the police to catch her killer was immense. The Met's investigation team turned to Paul Britton, a psychologist said to be the inspiration behind the TV series *Cracker*, starring Robbie Coltrane as Fitz, who would work alongside Greater Manchester Police to help them solve crimes.

Britton created a profile of the man he thought could have murdered Rachel. He believed her murderer was a sexually repressed loner who lived close to Wimbledon Common. He would be in his twenties or thirties with an interest in the occult and knives. The profile appeared to fit Colin Stagg. Police were so convinced that Stagg was the murderer, they took the extraordinary step of deploying an undercover female detective to entrap him and get him to admit to the killing.

The young policewoman, who used the alias Lizzie James, was brought in from Scotland Yard's covert operations unit SO15. She contacted him through a lonely hearts advertisement and attempted to get information by feigning a romantic interest in him, even enticing him into discussing violent sexual fantasies. At one point, Stagg told Lizzie he had fantasised about Rachel's killing, but he never admitted responsibility. Stagg would later say he only played along with Lizzie because he was interested in the romance. The police charged Stagg, but the case collapsed when the trial judge, Mr Justice Ognall, threw it out, saying the attempt to get Stagg to confess using a honeytrap was a 'deception of the grossest kind'.

Rachel Nickell's true killer, Robert Napper, was left at large to continue offending. In 1993, he broke into the home of 27-year-old Samantha Bisset in Plumstead and stabbed her eight times near her front door and dragged her into the lounge where he mutilated her body. Her four-year-old daughter, Jazmine, was woken by Napper in her bedroom. She was stripped and sexually assaulted, dressed again, and then smothered with a pillow. Napper was later caught in 1994 after fingerprints left at the scene were matched to him. A search of his flat found drawings and maps of different rape sites. Then in 2004, a forensics company called LGC would retest DNA found on Rachel's body and match it to Napper.

If the Nickell case was seen as a failure of *Cracker*-style psychologists and their ability to help with proper police work outside of a popular TV show, then the apprehension of John Duffy, the 'railway murderer', was considered one of its greatest triumphs. Duffy was a serial offender who attacked and raped women around London between 1982 and 1986. He would often carry out the attacks close to London's railway tracks with an accomplice called David Mulcahy.

Professor David Canter, a psychologist at the University of Surrey, was asked by the police investigation team to compile a psychological profile of the assailant. It was the first time in the UK that a university psychology department had worked with a police force to help them catch a killer using a systematic, empirically-based offender profile. Canter's work with the police was pre-dated only by a clinical assessment of Jack the Ripper in 1888 by the Queen's physician, Dr Thomas Bond, who argued, contrary to some expert opinion at the time, that the mutilations of the Ripper's victims were inflicted 'by a person who had no scientific nor anatomical knowledge . . . not even the technical knowledge of a butcher or horse slaughterer or any person accustomed to cut up dead animals'.

A century later, Canter worked with the police to create a profile of the railway murderer: married with no children, marriage problems, physically small, a martial artist who needed to dominate women and had bondage fantasies. Canter even managed to deduce where the suspect might live. Applying the profile, the police managed to narrow down their list of suspects from 2,000 to two. Duffy was one of the two.

The NCF was based at Bramshill House, the old police staff college near Basingstoke in Hampshire. For psychologists and behavioural science experts, the Wards' case was a chance to prove that their techniques could benefit major homicide inquiries, following the debacle of Rachel Nickell's murder inquiry. Cheshire Police was provided with a register of experienced psychologists and trained police officers at the NCF, and DS Simon Wells and Lee Rainbow had been chosen to provide Operation Menu with a 'second opinion'. Wells had fourteen years of experience as a detective. His colleague, Lee Rainbow, had been a behavioural science consultant with Surrey Police before taking a job at the NCF. He was tasked with providing police forces around the country with a range of behavioural advice, including crime scene assessment, case linkage analysis and predictive profiling. Rainbow was the real-life Cracker, the insightful outsider brought in to provide observations which might help the team think differently about the case.

Wells and Rainbow were given a verbal briefing by Operation Menu on 2 December 1999. They were given access to the case files and provided with the pathology photographs. They also visited Lacey Grove to get a 'feel' for the killings. The pair were instantly struck by how isolated the house was during the hours of darkness, echoing the concerns of Donald and Auriel's three sons, who had wanted their parents to move out of Lacey Grove for that very reason.

The two investigators considered how an attacker might have entered the house, and could not discount an assailant using a weapon to push their way into the Wards' property. The third-party offender, if one existed, had managed to avoid any interruption, and there was no evidence of gloves being used. The escape method was presumably via the kitchen door. They could see five types of weapon being used at the scene. The ceramic water bottle when it was intact; the water bottle's razor-sharp shards after it had been broken; the offender's bare hands; a pillow; and two kitchen knives.

They considered Donald and Auriel's injuries to be different in terms of their motivation. The attack on Auriel was 'expressive', while Donald's injuries were 'functional'. By expressive, they meant the violence inflicted upon Auriel went beyond the point of simply trying to end her life. The severity and prolonged nature of the attack inferred anger. The injuries sustained by Donald were more controlled. There was less emotion involved.

Rainbow and Wells examined the evidence around the

bloodstained keys in the kitchen door. If a third party was inside the house, they were likely to have exited by that door, but they were also likely to have entered using the same door. The question was – when did they enter the house? The alarm system probably precluded the possibility of the person staying overnight from the day before. The presence of the keys in the door raised a number of possible scenarios. The first possibility was a forced entry. The offender pushed their way inside using a weapon and had at least one of the Wards under their control. The second possibility was the attacker had let themselves into the house using their own key. The third possibility was that they were allowed to enter the house by either Donald or Auriel or both.

The first scenario was possible, but there was no sign of a struggle. Perhaps there wouldn't be. A quick shove in the doorway and the attacker would be inside the house. But why was Donald's blood in the key drawer? Could Donald have been attempting to escape the onslaught to run downstairs, before groping around in the drawer, forgetting that the key was in the kitchen door?

What about the second scenario? If an attacker had a key and entered the house, he could either leave the door unlocked or he could lock himself inside. But again, why the blood in the key drawer? Unless, of course, it was a skilful attempt to stage the scene. Staging, in policing terms, means an attempt to deliberately change a crime scene in order to misdirect the investigator. Again, this was possible. The NCF team could not rule it out based on the evidence from the scene, the police files and the pathology reports.

The third scenario: if either Donald or Auriel had let the

offender into their home, then one of them must have locked the offender inside and returned the key to the drawer. This may have happened in front of the offender, so he would know where the set of keys were kept, or, perhaps, had prior knowledge about where they kept their keys.

Their next consideration was the bedroom where the murder took place. Homicide investigations will always focus on the victim's body. Police know that in the vast majority of murders, the body is left where it drops. In the United States, a study of 5,224 homicides by Keppel and Weis (2004) using the Washington State Attorney General's homicide investigation and tracking system found only 1.3 per cent of murder victims had been placed in an unusual or awkward position, with 0.3 per cent posed and 0.1 per cent staged. There are several reasons why an offender might move, position or pose a body. It could be for sexual gratification. Or sadistic pleasure. It may be a contract killing designed to send a message.

The positioning of Donald's body was an issue for Rainbow and Wells. The dried blood pattern on Donald's face could not be explained by his final resting position. Donald was discovered looking upwards at the ceiling. So why did he have blood patterning on his face? The pattern was the sort which is imprinted only after sustained pressure with a bloodstained object. The most likely reason was that after Donald's throat was cut open, he was lying face down into the pillow while the wound haemorrhaged into the fabric of the pillow, causing the blood to imprint. Donald cutting his jugular vein would have meant a loss of consciousness in a short space of time. But if Donald was face down bleeding from a mortal wound, about to lose consciousness, how was he found staring up at the ceiling with a knife in his heart and a blood pattern on his face? It made no sense. Rainbow and Wells said that somebody had either moved Donald or had moved the pillow. The only question was: who?

The experts also had concerns about the method Donald had supposedly used to take his own life. Was it possible that Donald, who was right-handed, and had a wound to his right hand, sliced open his throat and stabbed himself in the chest? Was anyone physically capable of inflicting two such mortal wounds? Then there was the concerning lack of blood deposits on the wounds around Donald's body. This included a number of superficial cuts and stab marks to his groin and left wrist. He was bleeding from his hand, and yet there seemed to be no blood transferred from the wound to the other parts of his body. 'We are concerned that Mr Ward's wounds do not have significant blood deposits near to the other wounds, this needs further consideration,' they told the police in their report. Donald's blood on the key drawer and the knife drawer went some way to suggesting that he was the killer. But there was evidence which contradicted that conclusion. A third party could not be ruled out.

DCI Davis, the head of Operation Menu, would eventually produce a report for the coroner on his findings. In this report, Davis outlined why he believed Donald killed Auriel. 'It is my opinion, taking into account the results of an intensive investigation and the findings of all other agencies, that Donald Ward took his own life after killing his wife,' Davis wrote. 'The investigation has not revealed a motive or trigger incident for this act. However, it is clear that, at the time of his death, Donald Ward was under severe stress. I have produced a likely scenario, completed with the assistance of the other agencies and their findings.'

. A likely scenario. But was it the only scenario? Or was there another possibility? Was there a narrative that could better explain the blood staining on Donald's face? Or the lack of blood coming from the wounds around his body and the lack of staining from his bleeding hand? Or the way in which he managed to cut his throat and still have the strength to stab himself in the heart? Occam's Razor, the detective's mantra, is a compelling principle. The simplest explanation is often the right one – but not always.

The inquest was heard on 26 September 2000 by Cheshire's coroner, Nicholas Rheinberg. Rheinberg was an impressive performer in an inquest, robust, with a brilliant mind. As a result, he would preside over many of the more sensitive cases involving deaths in the prison services and the military, owing to his reputation for being a 'safe pair of hands'. But those who have witnessed a Rheinberg inquest will say that he comes into his own during the summing-up of the case at the end of the hearing. Colleagues will talk about him entering an almost 'trance-like state' while summarising weeks of complicated evidence, hardly needing to glance down at his carefully written notes.

During the evidence, Rheinberg heard nothing which could explain the reason for Donald killing his wife and himself. It was a mystery. 'This in all respects was so alien to Mr Ward's personality – his whole life – that not a single shred of evidence would suggest there was a time bomb waiting to explode,' he told the inquest. Based partly on evidence provided to him by

Operation Menu, Rheinberg recorded a verdict of unlawful killing in relation to Auriel. He found that Donald took his own life while the balance of his mind was disturbed for reasons unknown.

The Ainsworths get a brief mention in Davis's summary report, but they are not named. 'The reason that the door to the house was insecure and had apparently been unlocked by Donald Ward after he had received injuries is not clear,' he wrote. 'One potential explanation is that approximately eighteen months earlier, the deaths of two people who supported euthanasia occurred nearby. It was reported in the media at the time that persons intent on suicide were advised to leave their property insecure in order to facilitate access.'

The Ainsworths' deaths had actually occurred three and a half years earlier, not eighteen months. The methods used for the supposed euthanasia were also against the euthanasia society EXIT's principles, both in motive and methodology. After the inquest, Rheinberg wrote to Nigel Burgess, Chief Constable for Cheshire Police, to congratulate the police investigation and the 'meticulous care' with which the police file had been compiled. Davis was singled out for praise, saying he provided evidence at the inquest in a 'clear, concise, comprehensive and intelligent manner'. Indeed, there is no suggestion in this book from anybody that has been interviewed that he did otherwise, merely that the same facts can be open to different interpretation.

The four Wilmslow deaths present the same mystery. There was no rhyme or reason for the severity of the violence, which was entirely uncharacteristic of Howard or Donald. There was nothing in either of their relationships to suggest they might become killers and brutalise their partners. In the whole of the UK, between January 2000 and September 2019, there were thirty-nine couples over the age of sixty known to have died from murder-suicides. This works out to roughly two per year for a population of 66 million (rising from 58 million in 2000). Wilmslow, a town of 25,000 in the late '90s, had two such cases in three and a half years, making the deaths a statistical anomaly.

Christine Hurst placed the Wards' file in her 'Special Interest' box, where it sat with the Ainsworths' case and a number of other unusual deaths which had cropped up over the years. One of the other files in the box concerned a lady who had been murdered by her husband. Hurst once had a request from their son to view the file, but he had failed to show up at the police station at the appointed time. She kept it in the box, just in case he asked for it again. Other records in the box included the files relating to the deaths of Sally Clark's two children. Hurst felt this was the end of the road. She could see no other avenue in which the cases were going to be opened up and re-investigated.

Twelve weeks after the Wards were found dead in their dormer bungalow in Wilmslow, a third elderly couple were found dead. Once again, the police said they were victims of murder-suicide. This time, the couple lived in Didsbury, south Manchester, roughly seven miles away from Wilmslow. The husband was found by the police investigation to have murdered his wife and killed himself, despite his family insisting that his advanced Parkinson's disease meant he could hardly hold a cup of tea in one hand. No links were found between the three cases by the police. No patterns drawn.

The years went by. Christine Hurst would never forget those cases. But life went on. The cases kept coming in and the archives underneath Warrington Town Hall continued to swell with sudden and unexpected deaths in the county of Cheshire. The Wilmslow files would stay in Hurst's Special Interest box for another seventeen years, until they fell into the hands of an extraordinary investigator. And she was willing to sacrifice everything in her search for the truth.

I O

Ghosts of the Past

The rubbish-strewn sidewalk of East 13th Street in Manhattan, New York City, was already buzzing with activity when Stephanie Davies stepped out of the blue and white NYPD squad car with Detective Ed Dingman. Up ahead was a taped-off area. Detectives were interviewing witnesses; TV reporters were transmitting live reports from the street, their voices fast and urgent; and a crowd of curious pedestrians, mostly local residents who lived in the apartment blocks on the street, were collecting along the police cordon, trying to see what all the fuss was about. Some of the local residents were scared. There were rumours of a psycho on the loose. They wanted to know what the police were doing to make them safe in their homes.

It was June 2004. Davies, a forensic science student at Staffordshire University, was on a month-long attachment with Dingham, an NYPD detective. She was a graduate of forensic behavioural science at the University of Liverpool and had continued her academic studies in the field of forensics. She was in New York to get 'hands-on' experience of homicide investigation. And where better for crime scene experience than shadowing New York's finest over the course of a hot summer in the city?

A few days earlier, Davies had been in Pennsylvania, completing an advanced bloodstain-pattern analysis course, which involved watching the instructors whack pigs' heads with sledgehammers and then discussing the distribution of the blood spatter afterwards. Davies was fascinated by how blood spatter could be used to unlock the mysteries of a person's death and the clues its patterns could leave behind long after a person was murdered and she had travelled thousands of miles to develop her understanding.

A group of homicide detectives were already inside the cordon. Along the street was the detritus of the city's homeless. A discarded mattress. Sleeping bags. A mouldy rolled-up carpet. Flattened cardboard boxes. The news reporters were talking to Masha Chlenova, a graduate student, who said she no longer felt safe in her flat. 'I live here,' she said, pointing to the door of her apartment, a few yards away from the police cordon. 'It's really scary. Nobody knows what happened.'

Neither did NYPD's detectives. Yet. A steamer trunk had been found on the sidewalk with a woman's dead body inside. The trunk was three feet long, two feet high and two feet deep with a brass latch, and had been left standing upright between a chain-link fence, a rubbish bin and the corner of a building, so that it was partly hidden from view of the pedestrians who happened to be walking down 13th Street. The woman was stuffed inside like a rag doll, legs and arms at weird angles, the lid of the trunk shut tight and the trunk tied up with cables.

Davies followed Dingman under the cordon. They stood a few feet away from the trunk. Davies felt strangely calm about being at the centre of the whirlwind. She looked young for her age: baby-faced with bright blue eyes. At just over five feet, many of the male detectives towered above her. Her accent was rooted in the north-west of England with notes of Liverpudlian. She was surrounded by cops. Their voices had merged in one big soup of noise and activity.

Davies was born deaf. She had sensorineural hearing loss, which is when tiny cells inside the inner ear are not fully formed or are damaged. Since she was a toddler, she had taught herself to lip-read and how to assess people's body language. She had become adept at reading the subtle signs behind a person's posture and body movements. She wore hearing aids but they were not perfect, and she often needed to read a person's lips at the same time in order to understand fully what they were saying.

To some, such a disability might be regarded a weakness, making her unsuited to life as an investigator. Davies was different. She regarded it as one of her greatest strengths. Deafness had made her analytical. Focused. Observant. She was attuned to people, and yet detached from them. She knew her hearing would prevent her from ever joining the police as a law enforcement officer, but she stubbornly refused to view her deafness as an impediment and was determined to draw out its positives and use them to her advantage.

She watched the officers speak about the details of the case in their rapid-fire New York accents, their jargon, catchphrases and swearing all around her. She understood enough to gather that a homeless man called Edward Jones had come across a trunk in the street tied up with bungee cords and telephone wire. Jones opened it to discover the crumpled body of a 45-year-old woman, later identified as Myrna Gonzalez, a rough sleeper known to the authorities for her issues with drugs.

Davies was next to the trunk. The lid was open, but she was

standing on the other side of the case, with the lid blocking her view of the body. All she could see was the plastic sheet the body was wrapped in. 'She'll have been strangled,' she told Dingman in her typically blunt manner, a trait she blames on her Dutch heritage.

'Oh? Why do you think that?' said Dingman, confused for a moment.

'She's wrapped up in a trunk,' she said. 'That's personal. Strangulation is personal.'

Dingman, whose job at the NYPD was to provide forensic reviews of the crime scene, was astounded when the results of the post-mortem came back. The victim had a long history with the NYPD. She had been arrested no fewer than twenty-one times, including a couple of weeks before her body was found, for the theft of personal property. She struggled with drug addiction and had recently given birth to a girl named Nikia. The word Nikia was found by the pathologist tattooed onto her body. And Davies was right. She had been strangled. Years later a man would walk into a police station in the East Village and say he had strangled Gonzalez over an argument and that Jesus Christ wanted him to turn himself in.

Davies had always been intuitive. She had an instinctive feel for investigative work, aided by a prodigious memory and a keen eye for detail, attributes which would serve her well in her future career working for the Cheshire coroner.

Life hadn't always been easy for Davies. One of her first memories was gazing up at her parents, watching them look down at her, their lips opening and shutting like goldfish but no sound coming out. They would hold their arms out for hugs, but she would look back at them, confused and a little frightened. The world can be a scary place for a child born into silence.

Her father was a nuclear engineer. Her mother had been born in Amsterdam to Dutch parents but left Holland at eighteen. They had met while working on a P&O cruise liner. Stephanie was ten when her parents split up in 1989, and spent much of her youth and teenage years living with her mother in Wilmslow at a house in Lacey Green, just around the corner from the Wards' bungalow. She may well have rubbed shoulders with the Ainsworths and Wards in the town any number of times, but has no knowledge of ever having done so. Anneke, Davies' mother, even appears in the bundle of witness statements as part of Operation Menu, the police having knocked on her door to ask if she had seen anything suspicious. She could provide the police with nothing useful for their enquiries, but her statement was kept with the rest of the witness interviews.

School for Davies was a difficult experience at times. At primary school she wore radio aids, a hearing system which consisted of a transmitter worn by the teacher, and a receiver worn by Davies. The technology was designed to cut out the background noise and make the teacher's voice clearer so she could follow the lessons. It can also help deaf children develop their language skills. But while it may have helped her hear better, using it came with a social cost. She felt it alienated her from her peers. She sat in lessons with a black box strapped to her chest, the box in full view of her classmates.

When she was very young, her deafness had never felt like much of an issue. Children are adaptable, and she had never known any different. But strapping that box to her chest made her feel self-conscious. When she was nine, there was a boy in her class she really liked and wanted to make her friend. He had never paid her much attention. One day, though, her radio aids were taken away by the school staff for testing. The boy was amazed that she could understand him without her hearing-technology. For the very first time, he began to talk to her. Her heart soared. Finally, he was paying her some attention. But when the radio aids were returned and refitted an hour later, her new friend turned his back on her once more. Strange, but Davies would always remember that moment as a turning point in her life. She started to become angry and frustrated by her hearing problems. She was academically gifted, but her condition gave her a temper. It also made her tougher. She was an outsider, averse to the dangers of 'groupthink'.

When Stephanie was fifteen she started buying true-life crime magazines. One of them covered the murders carried out by Fred West, a serial killer who tortured and murdered at least twelve people for his own sexual gratification, with the help of his wife, Rose West, in Gloucestershire between 1967 and 1987. As a teenager Davies read David Canter's book *Criminal Shadows*, his account of his work in the field of criminal psychological profiling. Davies was fascinated by how psychological techniques could be used to catch the offender. To her, this was the detective work of the future.

At sixteen Stephanie was diagnosed with depression by the doctors at Kenmore Medical Centre. Her anger and frustration at her hearing problems continued throughout her teenage years, instilling a sense of perfectionism in her approach to her studies, fuelled by teachers and teaching assistants telling her what she would and would not be able to achieve as a deaf student. At the weekends she worked in a residential home called

Oakwood House, where she helped care for the residents. One day a man in his nineties was admitted. He was bitter at being made to live there. He was also angry about his hearing loss and was refusing to wear hearing aids. During one of his rants at the nursing staff, Davies, the youngest staff member by far, interjected. 'But I wear hearing aids and I'm only sixteen,' she said, turning her head to show him.

The man stopped and stared. He looked in turn at each of the staff members in the room, flabbergasted. 'Well, young lady,' he said finally. 'What an inspiration you are.' From that moment onwards, he wore his hearing aids without complaint.

Davies was regarded as a 'swot' at school, achieving good grades, but she also drank booze with the older kids from Lacey Green, meeting friends outside the Rex Cinema in Wilmslow town centre on a Friday night to walk down the hill and drink on the grassy banks of the River Bollin, listening to Guns N' Roses and Bon Jovi. When she was seventeen, she enrolled for a degree in psychology at Liverpool John Moores University, and began her studies in 1998. After finishing her degree, she studied for a masters in forensic behavioural science at the University of Liverpool, followed by another degree, this time in forensic science, at Staffordshire University, which she finished in 2005. Meanwhile, Davies contributed to academic papers on advanced crime scene investigation techniques and completed vocational courses in advanced bloodstain pattern analysis.

From a young age, Davies dreamed of joining the police and becoming a detective. But she knew her deafness would make it difficult. Modern police forces will usually accept recruits with hearing impairments so long as they can carry out the role of a police officer safely. They might be asked to complete a series of practical tests to assess the impact of the impairment on the person's communication skills. Davies knew her deafness would be considered too severe. But while studying for her forensic science degree at Staffordshire, she began to consider an alternative career as a coroner's officer. She researched the job and realised it would still give her the chance to investigate non-suspicious deaths, managing cases from their initial stages until their completion. If she couldn't be a detective, then this was the next best thing.

In November 2005, Davies wrote to Nicholas Rheinberg asking if she could shadow the coroner's officers based at Macclesfield Police Station. Rheinberg put her in touch with Christine Hurst, who gave Davies the chance to follow her around as she carried out her duties. There was an instant connection. Davies could see Hurst's passion for her work, striving every day to get the families the answers they needed. By then, Hurst was giving advice to the Home Office and Parliament about the coroner service in the wake of the Harold Shipman inquiry, which recommended tightening-up the system of death registration so that doctors couldn't simply sign off on medical cause of death without scrutiny. Weaknesses in the system had allowed Shipman to evade the authorities for years while killing indiscriminately in his role as a community doctor.

Davies started her first job as a coroner's officer at Thames Valley Police, working in High Wycombe, Buckinghamshire. She was thrown in at the deep end, dealing with families who had lost loved ones, taking their statements, identifying bodies in the mortuary, attending scenes of suicide and drug overdoses, sometimes in the middle of the night. Lack of resources and funding has seen the role of a coroner's officer become increasingly office-based, but back then she was investigating countless suicides while at Thames Valley Police, witnessing the scene of death first-hand. Dead bodies did not turn her stomach or give her nightmares. She would observe them in bedrooms, hospital beds and mortuaries with unemotional precision. 'Don't you find your job a bit depressing?' some of her friends would ask. She would tell them it had the opposite effect on her. It made her appreciate how precious life was, and why it was important to make every single day count.

Two years after she had shadowed Hurst, Davies saw an advert for a coroner's officer job with Cheshire Police. The job would mean she could live closer to her family and friends. After an interview by Rheinberg, Hurst and a police superintendent, she got the job, and started in April 2006, based with Hurst in Macclesfield. The team she joined were an eclectic bunch of former nurses, police officers and law graduates. No two people had the same background.

Shortly after Davies started, the team was relocated to Warrington Town Hall and moved into offices in its east annexe. The move was a big step down from Macclesfield 'nick'. The town hall was a grand-looking building, built in 1750 in landscaped gardens, four large white columns at its main entrance, a sweeping staircase up to the doors and a fine wrought-iron balustrade. Despite its impressive design, however, its listed status meant the council was severely restricted on what modifications it could make for the comfort of the staff working inside. The building was freezing cold in winter and boiling hot in summer. The east annexe flooded regularly, and water would leak into the IT equipment.

At the time, Davies was living with her father in Macclesfield.

She was excelling as a coroner's officer and had quickly become the stand-out investigator in the team. She was thorough, dedicated, and the bereaved families loved her. She adopted a caring attitude and would spend hours on the phone dealing with relatives, having long chats if they needed it, staying late after everybody else had left the office.

Hurst and Davies formed a strong team, and stuck together when the caseload built up. This was especially important in 2014, when rules around what deaths should be reported to the coroner were changed. Vulnerable people in hospitals and care homes who are deemed incapable of making decisions in their own best interest can have their freedom of choice taken away by the state. After 2014, people who were subject to such an order were reclassified as living in state care, meaning their deaths would be automatically referred to the coroner for investigation. They were known as Deprivation of Liberty (DoL) cases. Hurst and Davies faced an avalanche of casework, but they got through it together, as always.

On a fresh spring day in June 2013, Davies was sitting at her desk, hard at work on the latest deaths to come in. A cold breeze was sneaking in through the window in her office, which she shared with a retired detective inspector. He had a big booming voice. She didn't mind him, though. She had a loud voice too, so Hurst had put them in an office together so they could boom at each other. The window had been cracked ever since Davies had tried to push it open on a sweltering hot day the year before. The window had an ancient wooden frame, and in the process of trying to heave it up she had managed to break the glass. They'd alerted the council months ago, but nobody had come to fix it. In the end, Davies got used to the draught, and during the winter would sit at her computer with her coat on. In springtime the fresh air could be nicely cooling.

The window looked out on the town hall car park. Davies often saw groups of people leaving Warrington Magistrates' Court, the next building along from the town hall, to gather there for a fag or a spliff or to drink a bottle of lager. Once someone had looked out of the window to see a man masturbating in the middle of the car park. If the smokers were congregating underneath the window, Davies would sometimes shout out 'Could you smoke somewhere else, please? You're stinking out the office.' If they refused to move, she would go downstairs and challenge the groups of bemused, scruffily dressed men, who saw that, despite her small stature, she was not somebody to be trifled with. She was once assaulted by a man in Wilmslow who jumped out of a bush to paw at her chest. She grabbed her attacker and screamed 'F***k off!' in his face so loudly that he ran away from her. Davies chased him down the road shouting *'Get here now!'* He was lucky she never caught him.

The team of coroner's officers was based in three adjoining rooms in the east annexe. One of these belonged to Hurst, as the senior coroner's officer; the second to Davies and her retired-cop colleague; the third was where the rest of the coroner's officers sat. The coroner himself was based in a plush office in the west annexe, which had undergone several refurbishments over the years. A courtroom for inquest hearings was also in the west annexe.

Davies took a swig from her two-litre bottle of water. It was a permanent feature on her desk. She was fit and healthy and exercised regularly. Drinking the water was part of her strict routine. She wasn't a big tea-drinker. She preferred Pepsi Max or Diet Coke. On the more stressful days, she would crack through cans of Diet Coke like nobody's business. She had a 'Dead Fred' pen holder, a birthday present from a friend, a silicone rubber figurine in the shape of a dead person which could hold pens and pencils. She had to hide it in a drawer whenever a family member visited the office to give an interview or check documents. On the wall of her office, somebody had pinned up one of the causes of death given by a Cheshire GP: 'Death by exposure to cockatiels'. The person had died from bird fancier's lung, a type of hypersensitivity pneumonitis triggered by close proximity to avian proteins present in the droppings of some birds, such as cockatiels.

Davies looked up from her computer to see Hurst at the doorway. 'Got a minute?' said Hurst.

Davies nodded and followed her into her office. Hurst had requested her box of 'Special Interest' files out of archives. It had been in storage since the move from Macclesfield. Every inquest file had two versions in Cheshire – the original, which the coroner kept in the basement at Warrington Town Hall, and the coroner's officers' copy, stored in Cheshire Police's own archive system. The Criminal Justice Act 2009 meant inquest files could be disposed of after fifteen years. Until then, they were usually kept in the basement. Many files remained in the archives long after the required time.

Hurst took out the file for the Ainsworths, opened it up and looked at the crime scene photographs. Time had flown by for Hurst. She had got older. But Howard and Bea had never aged. They remained exactly the same. Two shocked faces in a bed covered in blood, a horrific moment frozen in time. Ghosts of the past.

Hurst knew all about Davies' academic and professional qualifications. She had a degree in psychology from Liverpool John Moores University, an MSC in forensic behavioural science from the University of Liverpool, a BSC (Hons) in forensic science from Staffordshire University, and would soon be conducting a PhD in psychological sciences at the University of Liverpool. She had professional qualifications in medico-legal death investigation, investigation of staged crime scenes, psychological autopsy investigation, advanced homicide investigation and criminal profiling and crime-scene analysis. She was a member of the Chartered Society of Forensic Sciences, the International Homicide Investigators Association, the Faculty of Forensic and Legal Medicine, the British Psychological Society and the Coroners' Officers and Staff Association. Davies would also become a guest lecturer in equivocal death investigation, crime scene interpretation and offender behaviour at scenes. Later in her career, she would provide Cheshire's trainee detectives with lectures concerning equivocal death and how to spot a staged crime scene.

The arrival of Davies had given Hurst an idea. In Davies, Hurst recognised a kindred spirit. Somebody with expertise that might provide insight into two cases she had never forgotten.

'Take a look at these photographs, will you?' Hurst said. 'They say he killed his wife.'

'When was this?'

'1996. Wilmslow.'

Hurst handed Davies a photograph. It was a colour image of

Howard and Bea lying side by side in their blood-soaked bed with its mustard-yellow headboard, yellow floral wallpaper with its repeating pattern of loops and swirls, the mint-green bed-sheets contrasting with the pool of crimson at Bea's side, their heads slightly turned towards one another, as if in conversation.

Davies examined the photo. Her first thought was that Bea was covered in blood. She had clearly been beaten with a blunt object multiple times and then stabbed in the head with a knife. Yet Howard's pyjamas were practically spotless.

'There's very little blood on his pyjamas,' Davies said. 'You'd expect to see more blood on his clothes if he carried out an attack with a hammer and a knife.'

Hurst nodded. At long last she had a member of staff on her team who had the knowledge, experience and qualifications to give credence to her suspicions. 'Anything else?'

Davies looked again, examining the bloodstains on Howard's pyjama top. 'The blood spatter looks wrong.'

'Why do you say that?'

'It doesn't look like impact spatter.'

Davies had been trained to recognise the shapes of blood-stains and what they could say about how they had come to land upon a surface, whether that be a wall, a floorboard, a piece of furniture or the victim themselves. The shape of bloodstains and the manner in which it lands on a surface can provide investigators with a great deal of information. An attacker who has wielded a hammer or a knife is likely to have blood drop-lets land on them which look like spots with tails, almost like tadpoles. This not only shows directionality, but that they have landed with force. The blood droplets will have been moving quickly through the air before impacting upon a surface.

The precious few droplets of blood present on Howard's top looked nothing like that. These spots were large and circular in shape. Davies recognised the spatter to be passive. This happens when the force propelling the droplets through the air is gravity alone. They had landed on Howard's pyjama top at a ninety-degree angle, meaning he was likely to have been lying down on the bed at the time Bea was attacked. It suggested to Davies that Howard was killed first.

Davies quickly scanned the post-mortem reports which came with the file. She had never seen violence like it in a domestic.

'It's seventeen years since I was the coroner's officer for this case,' Hurst said. 'I never believed Howard Ainsworth could have done that to his wife. He wasn't the type. He was a quiet and gentle old man. They put it down to euthanasia and death with dignity. I don't see much dignity there, do you? I warned the police at the time. But they didn't listen.' There was a second file sitting on Hurst's desk.

'What's that?' Davies said, nodding at the file.

Hurst picked it up. 'Another murder-suicide. Three years later in Wilmslow, the same thing happened again.'

'You're *joking*.'

Hurst smiled. It reminded her of her exact reaction with Dave Bourne all those years ago in the mortuary when he had pulled out the tier containing Auriel Ward on the bottom tray.

'Elderly couple. Husband and wife. Found dead side by side in their bed.'

Davies stared at her in a moment of disbelief. She took the file from Hurst. The Wards' file was incomplete. It contained no photographs of the crime scene, and much of the documentation was missing. However, it did contain the post-mortem reports by the two pathologists, the first by Dr Johnson, hours after the bodies were discovered, the second three weeks later by Dr Williams, carried out by order of the coroner. Hurst read out Auriel's injuries. Davies was amazed. The attack on Auriel was almost identical to the attack inflicted upon Bea: strangling and blunt-force trauma, ending with injuries from a sharp instrument. Even the positions of the bodies in the bed sounded the same.

'I've never been happy with these cases,' Hurst said. 'That's why I've kept them in that box. I wanted to know where they were, just in case. I think they're linked.'

She told Davies about raising her concerns with both police investigations at the time, and how nothing had come of it. Hurst said she had been worried by the lack of forensic examination carried out on Howard and Bea Ainsworth. She thought it could have potentially led to some important evidence being missed.

Davies hadn't seen enough of the evidence yet to form a proper conclusion, but she trusted Hurst's instincts. It wouldn't be the first time Hurst had reported patterns of suspicious deaths to the police and got it right. She knew what Hurst was proposing and was staggered by the enormity of it. It would mean innocent men had been blamed for the murders of their loved ones. Murders which the coroners in each case had described as 'inexplicable', but then gone on to agree with the findings of the police. In other words, Hurst was telling her that the wrong people had been blamed all those years ago, and the real killer was yet to be found.

11

Pandora's Box

A deafening roar ripped through Bosley, a small village nestled in the south-east corner of Cheshire beside the Bosley Cloud, a hill on the border of the Peak District which arches across green fields like the hump of a cresting whale. The very pavements in Bosley trembled. Windowpanes shattered in the houses and shops. Car alarms went off. Dogs and cats darted for cover and birds left the trees for the safety of the sky. It was 9.10 a.m. on Friday, 17 July 2015. The terrified residents of Bosley, population 400, ran from their homes and stood on their doorsteps to see a giant fireball rising above the wood-treatment mill in the village.

The blast was caused by a massive explosion of wood dust, a highly flammable and explosive material. Four mill workers died in the explosion. The police launched a major investigation into the causes of the accident. Meanwhile, Cheshire's coroner's officers were left with a huge task on their hands. Bodies had to be identified. Families had to be informed. Inquests had to be arranged. Stephanie Davies was assigned coroner's officer for the Bosley explosion. She had recently been promoted to the position of assistant senior coroner's officer, working as Christine Hurst's deputy.

A week after the explosion, Davies visited the Bosley mill

site with Nicholas Rheinberg, the Cheshire coroner. They walked about the mill in protective clothing, escorted by police officers. The fires were burning, even then. Rubble was strewn about. It reminded Davies of being at Ground Zero in New York. The earth had that same scorched look to it. Davies and Rheinberg met with the search and rescue team to discuss how to proceed. There was much to do.

They needed a search strategy in order to identify the human tissue of the four victims. Davies would work with the police liaison officers and keep the families of the victims in the loop on the recovery of the bodies. It was tough, detailed work. She excelled at it, and in 2015 was awarded a commendation by the chief constable for her contribution to the Bosley inquiry. It was one of several awards she would win for her work as a coroner's officer at Cheshire Police, including the Chief Constable's Commendation in 2020 for professional service provided to the county of Cheshire, as well as an award for work she would later carry out during the Covid pandemic. At the time, Davies was in near-constant contact with the detectives assigned to the Bosley investigation. A new bone found at the site. Call Davies. Some human tissue identified. Call Davies. Scraps of clothes found. Call Davies. When leaving one of the endless Bosley briefings, Davies told a detective that, once Bosley was finished, there might be an interesting pair of cases in Wilmslow worth re-examining.

'How come?' the detective asked.

'My boss thinks there could be a killer on the loose in Cheshire who got away with murdering two elderly couples,' she said. 'Why, are you interested?'

'Maybe. But don't you think we're busy enough as it is, Steph, without a serial killer on the loose?'

They laughed. Davies was gently testing the water. She hadn't looked at the files in detail. But Hurst's theory had lodged itself in her head. What if she was right? What if those cases were linked and nobody had bothered to look at them properly? Occasionally, Davies and Hurst might discuss the Wilmslow killings over lunch or a coffee. Davies always promised to take a proper look at them one day and sift through the evidence. But their day jobs were busy, and the hours could be extremely demanding. There was never any time. The months and years slipped by. Davies bought a house in Warrington closer to her workplace to cut down on her commute.

She signed up to fight in a pink-collar boxing match for charity. She won the fight, but afterwards developed sciatica and was told by the doctors that she would never be able to run or do Thai boxing again, a hobby she enjoyed for stress relief. She ignored the doctors and carried on with her boxing. Meanwhile, she split up with her long-term partner and best friend, Adam, feeling the relationship was not progressing. They had met in the Blue Lamp pub in Wilmslow, which no longer exists, when she was twenty and Adam almost nineteen. His parents owned an Italian restaurant in the town. They had an on-off relationship but had been steady for the last six years before they split up. There was no dramatic reason for the separation. Over the years they had simply drifted apart.

Hurst, meanwhile, was putting some serious thought into retiring. She had broached the topic with Nicholas Rheinberg. Rheinberg was on the brink of retiring from his role, too, so he persuaded her to stay on a little longer so they could leave together. They had enjoyed a close working relationship for decades, both of them inquiring into tens of thousands of deaths in Cheshire during their time. They understood one another. He didn't want to lose his chief investigator and get in somebody new just before the end. Hurst agreed out of loyalty to Rheinberg and extended her service. Rheinberg's last day was 10 March 2017. Hurst left two weeks later.

Rheinberg's replacement was Alan Moore, a former colonel in Army Legal Services, who had seen tours with the British Army from Ireland to Iraq, and worked at the United Nations and the Ministry of Defence. Moore was already deputy to the senior coroner, so the team knew him well. Like Rheinberg before him, Moore would bring his own methods and ideas about how he wanted the coroner's office to function. The haunting spectre of Harold Shipman had never quite left Rheinberg, nor indeed any coroner of his generation, and he had always erred on the side of caution, even if it meant dealing with a higher caseload. Moore wanted to streamline the number of deaths reported to the team, particularly deaths reported by hospitals or GPs. It brought down the number of deaths being reported from 5,000 a year to roughly 3,000, with the number of inquests remaining steady at 700–800 a year.

Christine Hurst's departure was a huge blow to the coroner service, not just in Cheshire but nationally. She had spent twenty-four years as a coroner's officer for Cheshire Police, nineteen of them as the senior coroner's officer. By the time of her departure, she had personally investigated 12,000 deaths in the county of Cheshire, while teams under her supervision would have investigated more than 75,000 deaths during that time. She left the force with an exemplary record, recognised as one of the most experienced coroner's officers in the country, who had advised the government on reforming the service and designed medical courses to help train other officers around the UK.

Stephanie Davies was the natural choice to take over from Hurst. In 2017, she was appointed senior coroner's officer by Cheshire Police, and made personally responsible for a team which had expanded to fourteen people, including a deputy manager, eleven coroner's officers and two administrative support staff. Her job was to oversee all deaths coming through to the department, monitoring suicides, child deaths, prison deaths and forensic post-mortems for senior police officers and public health. She would also provide training for police officers and detectives, and represent the department at senior leadership meetings.

For the first time, Davies would be exposed to the cut and thrust of politics inside Cheshire Police. The workload was huge. But like Hurst, she was passionate about the job, and would do everything in her power to make sure the bereaved families that went through her department would be provided with the answers they deserved. Davies and Hurst may have had a close bond, but in many ways they were completely different. Where Hurst was calm and cautious, Davies was fiery and daring. Davies was a risk taker. Even at school she was known for her rebellious streak, which she always put down to her deafness. Her condition made her different. It meant she had to fight twice as hard to get what she wanted. It made her blunt with her peers. She wasn't afraid to tell people when she thought they were wrong. But more than anything, for Davies, it was about the families, and getting the answers they deserved. The job was about them.

*

The month of July 2018 would bring good news for Stephanie Davies. The College of Policing wrote to inform her it would fund her doctorate at the University of Liverpool. Her PhD was to carry out research into equivocal death, or, in other words, deaths considered ambiguous by the police and coroner. It was a prestigious bursary to receive. Hundreds apply each year. Few are successful. The college was particularly interested in her focus on staged deaths, or disguised murders.

Academics in the United States have carried out some research in the field. A 2012 paper called 'Crime Scene Staging in Homicide' was published in the respected *Journal of Police and Criminal Psychology*. The paper was written by Professor Louis Schlesinger, from the Department of Forensic Psychology at the John Jay College of Criminal Justice in New York, his fellow academics at the college, Ashley Gardenier and Jamie Sheehan-Cook, and John Jarvis from the FBI's behavioural science unit. Their research took a sample of 946 homicides, supplied by the FBI for the purposes of the study. Their idea was to examine the murders in order to determine the prevalence of 'stagers', which in this context was murderers who had used methods to steer the investigation away from themselves as the logical suspects. For example, the offender physically changes the scene to make a domestic homicide appear to be an accident, or make a murder look like a suicide by leaving a note, or a murder seem like a robbery gone wrong by removing valuable items.

The results of Schlesinger's study found that in the 946 homicide crime scenes, staging had occurred in 79 (8.35 per cent) of the cases. Out of the staged group, the most prevalent staging method was arson, found in twenty cases. Verbal staging, or lying to police, occurred in seventeen cases, while fourteen cases were staged as burglary, robbery, or breaking and entering. There were eleven murders staged as accidents, which included automobile accidents or falls.

One of those eleven supposed accidents was a case involving a woman who had severely beaten her mother to death. Before the police arrived, she washed her mother's body, changed her clothes, and placed her body at the bottom of the staircase to make it look as though she had fallen to her death in a freak accident. There were six homicides staged to look like suicides. In one case, a man had shot his girlfriend in the head after she had laughed at him during target practice. He had placed a gun in the victim's hand and pointed the gun at her head in order to make it appear as if she had shot herself.

Researchers also came across four cases of staged murder-suicides. One of them was a man who shot his father and brother. The brother was shot four times in the head, the father shot in the head once. The murderer put the gun in his father's hand and told the police he thought his father had killed his brother and committed suicide. The study found one case where the murderer had carried out body posing in order to satisfy their perverse sexual fantasies, which is also classed as a form of crime scene staging. The case involved a husband who killed his wife by suffocation with a pillow. He then unbuttoned, unzipped and pulled down her trousers, exposing her underwear. He lifted up her shirt and removed her bra. She had not been sexually assaulted, according to the study.

A second influential paper on crime scene staging was published in 2014, again in the United States. 'Staged Crime Scenes: Crime Scene Clues to Suspect Misdirection of the

Investigation' was authored by Arthur S. Chancellor, a special agent for the US Army's investigations unit based out of Fort Bragg, North Carolina, and Grant Graham, the forensic manager for Fayetteville Police Department in North Carolina. Chancellor was one of US law enforcement's most respected investigators, who formed part of the inquiry team which investigated the 1995 Oklahoma terrorist bombing, working for the US Department of Justice.

Chancellor's study found that offenders who stage a scene often make a mistake by presenting too much evidence for investigators to find, a trait he called 'exaggeration'. One very simple example is when an offender wants to make a murder look like a suicide. The victim is shot in the head and a gun placed into the victim's hand. The killer thinks that is what the police would expect to find in such a situation because they have never seen a crime scene like that before.

Chancellor said that in those types of scenes, however, the gun is often not found in the victim's hand. It is usually found in the *vicinity* of the victim, where it has been dropped after the trigger has been pulled. This is an example of the offender trying too hard to mask their crime. Another recognisable example of staging, he found, was depersonalisation, which he defines as 'the actions taken by a murderer to obscure the personal identity of the victim'. The head and face may be beaten beyond recognition, or the face might be covered with an object, such as a pillow. Once the face is covered, the victim is transformed into an anonymous body, which is easier for the offender to deal with psychologically.

Davies proposed a theory which the College of Policing were keen for her to research. She believed that offenders in the

UK were altering crime scenes more than the police realised, something she called the '*CSI* effect', after the long-running American crime drama, which follows a team of crime scene investigators as they use physical evidence to solve murders. Davies believed that our consumption of TV cop shows, films and documentaries means the public is more aware than ever before of the various techniques available to catch an offender. DNA. Fingerprints. Hair. Blood. All valuable clues for modern science to investigate.

Davies was about to embark on a doctorate in equivocal death. And there were no deaths more open to interpretation, in her view, than the Wilmslow killings Hurst had once shown her in her office one afternoon several years ago. One quiet evening in the office in April 2018, Davies decided to open up Hurst's box of Special Interest files, which was being kept in a locked cupboard in the office. She found the coroner's files relating to the deaths of Howard and Bea Ainsworth, and Donald and Auriel Ward, and took them home with her. She started the laborious process of reading through bundles of witness statements, post-mortem examination documents and expert reports.

Davies knew there would be more material on both cases in the archives, so that week she contacted the archivist at Warrington Town Hall, who looked after the stacks of records in the basement. Each file had a reference number, but according to the archivist there was no reference for the Ainsworths on the computer system. There was a chance it had been destroyed – by law they only had to keep the file for fifteen years. But Davies had a strange feeling it was still in the basement. Somewhere in the dust, damp and cobwebs.

The archives were underneath the west annexe of Warrington Town Hall. Davies unlocked the door at the side of the town hall building and went through to a second door. She opened it and walked down a flight of dusty old stone steps. It was pitch black in the basement. She scrabbled to find the light. She flicked the switch and lit up the room. Nobody visited this place except for the archivist. It had been flooded several times and damp had seeped into the walls. The archives consisted of rows and rows of boxes stacked on shelves, and within those boxes were files on people who had died unexpectedly or suddenly in the county of Cheshire. The inquest files were in numbered order by year; the non-inquest files were stored separately. Some of the files were simply bundles of papers tied in the top-left corner. Files with photographs were kept in big brown envelopes. Davies felt in awe. She wanted to sit and read through all the historic cases. Her doctorate would mean spending an awful lot of time in this basement, searching through the files. Most people would dread such a task. Davies was thrilled by it. Who knew what secrets she might unlock?

She had a reference number for the Wards. She found the file stored in the correct location. The brown envelope was marked: DONALD + AURIEL WARD 79/80 − YEAR 1999 MACC PLEASE ADD TO BOX 01/05/04/00052/99. She started searching for the Ainsworths' file. She spent hours picking through those shelves, opening box after box, but without a reference number it was like looking for a needle in a haystack. She was about to give up when she came across a box labelled 1987. It was sitting on a bench in the basement, completely out of place. Even though it was the wrong year, something compelled her to open it. She opened the lid.

I don't believe it, she thought. On top of the pile was a brown envelope.

HOWARD ✝ FLORENCE BEATRICE AINSWORTH PLEASE PLACE IN BOX NUMBER – 01/05/04/00004/95. She had what she needed to begin a full review of the Wilmslow killings. The full title of the confidential report she would eventually produce for the major incident team (MIT) at Cheshire Police was 'Case Reviews: Wilmslow murder suicides'. But inside Cheshire Police headquarters, senior officers would refer to it simply as the 'Davies Review'.

1 2

The Review: Ainsworths

At the top of the first page of the Davies Review is an executive summary which acknowledges the efforts of the original police inquiries. 'It is certainly not the intention to bring into disrepute the findings of those original investigators who worked on these cases twenty years ago,' Davies wrote. 'The knowledge that investigators have these days surrounding forensics, bloodstain pattern analysis and crime scene interpretation is more advanced compared to twenty years ago.'

The report begins with the Ainsworths, providing a brief biography of their lives, along with a summary of the original police investigation. 'Early on, with the presence of suicide notes and the membership to the euthanasia society, initial appearances were that Mr Ainsworth had killed his wife and then taken his own life,' Davies wrote. 'Additional checks were done which supported this hypothesis (handwriting analysis, euthanasia documents, interview with son). On this basis the case was treated as a murder-suicide, and no one else was thought to be connected to the deaths.'

The section on the Ainsworths contains a series of colour photographs. 'The photographs depict the couple lying deceased in their nightclothes on the bed,' Davies went on.

Blood spatter and loss of blood is clearly apparent from Mrs Ainsworth, indicating she was attacked and died on the bed. Mr Ainsworth can be seen with a plastic bag on his head, has dried layer urine stains on his pyjama bottoms and a small number of bloodstains on his pyjamas. Mrs Ainsworth has a bloodstained pillow covering her face and a knife protruding from the centre of the pillow. She has lost blood and appears to have been incontinent of urine. She has what appear to be fresh abrasions on her knees, and faint fresh bruises on her right shin. Her nightdress appears to have been pulled up, exposing her genital area.

There was no mention in the coroner's file, Davies noted, of the plastic bag, hammers or knife being fingerprinted.

Her first observation focused on Howard's left hand and arm, which were trapped under his body in an uncomfortable-looking position. Howard's head was propped up unnaturally against the headboard. In her view, his posture was not consistent with a final resting position. 'This position is more consistent with his body having been moved, or rearranged, after death,' she wrote.

She noticed from the mortuary pictures a patch of 'blanched lividity' next to his buttock. Lividity is when the skin turns reddish to bluish purple due to the settling and pooling of blood following death. Gravity begins to take hold, and everything sinks to its lowest point. Most of Howard's leg and side were purple. But his buttock showed a patch of white where his hand had been resting. She believed this was likely to have been caused by Howard being picked up and put down, trapping his hand between his buttock and the mattress, causing the white mark.

If Howard's final position was strange, then Bea's was quite extraordinary, suggestive of a killer who wanted to degrade and humiliate her in her final moments. 'Mrs Ainsworth's nightdress appears to have been deliberately pulled up on one side,' Davies wrote. 'In addition, her face has been deliberately covered up.' Her nightdress being yanked up, and her face being deliberately covered was, according to Davies, evidence of 'signature behaviour', where actions at the scene are carried out by the offender in order to meet a psychological or fantasy-based need.

Bea had abrasions and bruising to her knees and her right shin. 'They were caused recently [the abrasions] and are consistent with either a fall or drag across a semi-rough surface, such as carpet.' It was 'suggestive' that at some point she had tried to get away and was dragged back by the offender, the report said. 'This could also indicate she was not asleep or unconscious prior to when the attack started.'

One of Davies' areas of expertise was in bloodstain pattern analysis: she had not only studied it at degree level, but also attended career development courses to further her professional knowledge of the field. She was trained to interpret blood and how it behaves when it falls, according to a specific set of pre-determined scientific principles. Those principles can allow bloodstain pattern analysts to examine blood evidence left behind and draw conclusions about how it may have been shed.

To the casual eye, bloodstains at a crime scene might appear random. But modern forensic experts can now help detectives recreate the sequence of events for the crime by gathering information from spatter patterns, transfers and voids (the blank spaces underneath a body). Davies understood how the size, shape, distribution and location of certain bloodstains could help unlock the secrets of how an attacker behaved during their assault. She could analyse the physics of how blood behaved when spattered, and the mathematics of its behaviour. Her analysis of the blood spatter in the Ainsworths' bedroom took into account the headboard, the wall above the headboard, the pillow beneath Bea's head, the blood on Bea's nightdress, the blood on Howard's pyjamas, the blood on the wall adjacent to the bed, the blood on the suicide note, the drops on the bedding on the left- and right-hand side of Howard's legs and the plastic bag on Howard's head.

She believed the blood spatter on the headboard was radi-ating impact spatter coming from Auriel. 'This will have been caused when Mrs Ainsworth was attacked,' wrote Davies. Radiating impact spatter is blood which has radiated outwards due to the force of impact, travelling at medium-high velocity. Davies thought that the direction the blood had travelled, so high up the headboard, meant Bea was likely to have been sitting up at the time of the attack. 'It is not cer-tain if she was sitting up or lying down at the time she was attacked,' Davies wrote. 'However, using the directionality of the spatter depicted in the photographs, the approximate area of origin would suggest she was sitting up at the time of the attack.'

Next, she considered Howard's clothing, something which had concerned Hurst back in 1996. 'If Mr Ainsworth had attacked his wife, there should be significantly more blood-staining and spatter present on his clothing,' she wrote.

There was no bloodstained clothing found anywhere at the scene, nor in the rubbish. There was also no evidence that he got changed after the death of his wife. This is strongly suggestive that any bloodstained clothing had been removed from the house prior to the discovery of the deaths. This is also inconsistent with Mr Ainsworth having been the person who attacked his wife.

The droplets on his pyjama top did not show the 'directionality' expected had the blood spatter come from Bea while Howard was supposedly pummelling her with a hammer. Such an attack would create droplets with impact velocity. In layman's terms, impact velocity would make droplets with small tails, rather than round blobs, which are passive spatter. 'If Mr Ainsworth had carried out the attack on his wife, more impact spatter should have projected back onto his clothing,' Davies wrote. 'The linear, medium-large circular stains on the pyjama bottoms are indicative of: i) landing on the pyjamas at an approximate ninety-degree angle (i.e. perpendicular); ii) gravitational pull (especially with the larger-sized stains).' In other words, the blood flew up into the air and fell back down onto Howard, rather than flew at him directly with force.

'Significantly', Davies added, 'this strongly suggests that at the time that Mrs Ainsworth was attacked with the blunt-force object, Mr Ainsworth was actually lying nearby, in a supine position.' In her view, due to the severity and prolonged nature of the attack using multiple weapons, causing Bea to have severe blood loss, it was not possible for Howard to have been the killer and have so little blood on his clothes, or, indeed, so little blood on his right hand, which he would have used to wield the hammer and the knife. There was evidence that Howard had not washed his hands, meaning the lack of blood could not be accounted for by a quick clean-up in the sink. Davies found spots of blood on his right thumb and index finger which would not have been present had his hands been washed.

Davies spotted the presence of bloodstains on the bedding either side of Howard, which she described as 'cast-off stains'. 'It is not entirely clear if at this time Mr Ainsworth was originally lying on the floor, or on the bed,' she wrote. 'Given there are similar stains seen on the bedsheets either side of Mr Ainsworth, it is more likely than not that he was lying on the bed at the time of Mrs Ainsworth's attack.' She noted it would have been 'helpful' had the bed been photographed after Howard's body was removed. 'The absence of blood on the bed (i.e. showing a voided area) would have confirmed if he was indeed lying there at the time Mrs Ainsworth was attacked,' she said.

The plastic bag on Howard's head also provided Davies with valuable insight into how he may have died. On close inspection, Davies identified blood spatter on the bag which she regarded to be impact spatter, matching the staining on the headboard. 'This is strongly suggestive that the plastic bag was *in situ* on Mr Ainsworth's head at the time Mrs Ainsworth was attacked,' she wrote.

On the wall adjacent to the bed, which featured the yellow wallpaper, was 'swing cast-off spatter', possibly from a hammer swinging backwards, splashing blood against the wall. On a ligature found on the bedroom floor, Davies noticed a small blood transfer pattern, created when a wet, bloody surface comes into contact with a secondary surface. 'Could this be a fingerprint belonging to the offender?' she surmised. 'If this item is still in police archive, could this fingerprint be compared via the Automated Fingerprint Identification System (AFIS)?'

The key items used in the attack were the hammer in the sink, the hammer in the bedroom, the knife, the plastic bag with ligature attached and the second ligature on the bedroom floor. Davies believed the hammer in the sink was likely to have been the weapon used to bludgeon Bea around the head. She found evidence of diluted blood circling the plug hole, indicating the hammer had been washed after being used on Bea. 'Washing a weapon is MO behaviour [method of carrying out the crime and getting away with it] in order to remove forensic evidence,' she wrote. 'If Mr Ainsworth was planning to take his own life, why bother washing the hammer?'

The second hammer left in the bedroom did not appear to have been used by the offender. 'This object is alien to this scene,' wrote Davies. 'This indicates that the offender brought it to the scene. This, along with the introduction of the other hammer and knife, shows evidence of planning. These weapons also contradict the planned methodology described in the handwritten notes.'

Her report showed a photograph of the knife that was found in Bea's head. 'It appears to show the knife tip has broken off,' she said, 'indicating it has been impaled with significant force (forensic tests confirmed it was not struck by either hammer).' It meant the attacker would have to be strong enough to stab somebody through the forehead and past the skull, pushing the blade deeper once the blow was struck. The lack of defence injuries on Bea's hands or arms possibly meant she became unconscious quickly or was simply unable to defend herself, Davies said.

'Given the abrasions on her knees and that the impact spatter indicated she was sat up,' Davies wrote, 'it is very unlikely she was asleep when she was first attacked.' Another area of concern for Davies was the two deep purple marks on either side of Howard's upper lip. She noted the post-mortem findings which stated: 'There are injuries to the lips that are not explained by this [plastic bag] mechanism.' In Davies' opinion, they were injuries more commonly seen in homicidal smothering cases. 'They are not found in suicide cases,' she wrote.

Davies went through the evidence produced by the police investigation's toxicology report. The photographs showed a 'medication bottle' in front of the TV in the bedroom, along with 'two small whisky glasses'. The medication was Heminevrin (chlormethiazole), a hypnotic drug used for people with alcohol dependency. It was not prescribed to either of the Ainsworths. The bottle was labelled as containing twenty-eight tablets and twenty-two were present, meaning six were missing. 'The toxicology analysis did not detect this drug in the toxicology screen for both Mr and Mrs Ainsworth,' Davies wrote. 'It has never been established how this medication got into the property. Nor is there any evidence that the bottle was tested for fingerprints.'

'It is worth bearing in mind, however,' she added, 'that chlormethiazole does have a shorter half-life compared to similar hypnotics/benzodiazepines. However, the forensic scientist's analysis on the pills states that the metabolites should still be detectable in the urine, even if the parent drug had been broken down in the blood. Laboratories in 1996 should have had the facilities to test for this drug,' she went on, 'especially if they were informed it was present at the scene.' The toxicology reports attached to the post-mortem reports in the coroner's file do not state the full range and sensitivity of the testing. 'However, had this drug been detected, this still does not exclude forceful administration by a third party, or voluntary self-administration if the person was under duress.'

The suicide letter and the note containing the Ainsworths' son's address appeared to have been laid out in the bedroom prior to Bea being attacked, Davies said. This was due to blood spatter being evident on the paper, blood which lay on top of the ink lettering. 'This indicates the events as being planned,' she wrote, 'rather than being an act of impulse'.

She turned to the content of the letter. It was an important piece of evidence which had swayed the police inquiry team towards Howard being his wife's murderer. Davies had read dozens of suicide notes during her time as a coroner's officer in the counties of Buckinghamshire and Cheshire. She had never come across a suicide letter like this one. 'The terminology does not seem consistent with the style of writing that is generally seen in suicide notes,' she said.

Suicide notes are a chance for the deceased to have their last words, to explain to loved ones the reasons behind their decision, and to provide instructional information such as funeral arrangements and who they want certain possessions to go to. But much of this suicide letter was a description of Bea's symptoms and the logistics around the visit of the GP. 'The author has dealt with many suicide cases throughout her career, and she has viewed many notes that were left by the deceased and were accepted as evidence of suicidal intent at inquest hearings,' Davies wrote. 'These notes would be left behind for the family, loved one or they were warnings to finders to call the police. The terminology in this note is confusing, contradictory and filled with extraneous information.'

The suicide letter contained a description of how Howard was supposedly going to murder his wife: 'It looks as tho our lives have gone so have given her some sleeping tablets and I will have to throttle her as she would [not] be able to use the bag method.' But no pills were found in her system. And Bea was murdered using a ligature, a hammer and a knife. The circumstances of the death did not reflect what the note said was going to happen.

The long-winded sentence structure was also unusual, since in moments of such heightened emotion, it has been proven in suicide note authenticity studies, bona fide notes tend to use shorter sentence structures rather than long sentences (Jones and Bennell, 2007). 'It was as if the writer was trying to think of ideas on what to write,' Davies wrote, 'or to take his time writing the note, rather than leave a clear and concise message behind for loved ones.' She also questioned the lack of emotion. Suicide letters usually express strong emotion, either positive or negative. This one was strangely emotionless and factual.

The Davies Review posed a number of questions. Did Howard have the physical strength to carry out an attack of this nature on his wife? Did his personality type make him capable of such an act? After all, there was no history of mental illness, domestic violence or marital problems. They were described by friends and family as a 'devoted couple'. Howard was a gentle giant, a lover of birds and nature. He believed in euthanasia, but contacting the GP surely indicated a desire for his wife's condition to improve, rather than a desire for her to die. The explanation of euthanasia as a rationale for murder didn't make

sense. 'Euthanasia supporters are more likely to employ sedative drugs and asphyxiation as a chosen methodology,' wrote
Davies. 'The society [SVES] did not condone the use of violence
or knives for "self-deliverance".' She said the society advised
members to take sedative drugs in conjunction with the bag
method. 'In their experience if used without sedative drugs,'
she wrote, 'the person is likely to thrash about and attempt to
pull the bag off, failing in their suicide attempt.'

Davies found Bea's injuries to be inconsistent with the methods employed by euthanasia supporters, who believed in 'death
with dignity'. Instead, she recognised signs of signature behaviour, meaning the killer may have had a psychological need to
inflict pain on their victim. Bea sustained far more injuries than
necessary to cause her death. Overkill, Davies said, was caused
by cumulative rage taken out on the victim. 'Her injuries were
expressive as opposed to instrumental, indicating the offender
was expressing an intense rage at the victim,' she wrote. The
significant blunt-force blows on her head were indicative of
'anger-retaliatory signature'. The blunt-force trauma, or the
hammer blows on her head, represented the need to control
and dominate the victim. The insertion of the knife into the
brain could be of 'paraphilic' origin, a condition characterised
by abnormal sexual desires, typically involving extreme or
dangerous activities, and represented sexual domination over
the victim. 'While there may not have been overt signs of any
sexual abuse on the female,' wrote Davies, 'her murder may
have acted as a sexual release for the offender, as well as a way
to finally release his built-up anger and frustration.'

The covering of Bea's face with the pillow was a form of
depersonalisation, when the offender transforms the victim

into an object that is no longer human. It would stop Bea 'seeing' the offender leave the scene. Finally, leaving her pubic area exposed was a form of humiliation, a way to degrade the victim, Davies said. In contrast, Howard's injuries were instrumental: in other words, the aim was to reach death quickly, with little emotion behind the attack.

Davies saw nothing in the Ainsworths' past, or in the testimony of their friends and family, which suggested Howard would want to kill Bea in such a way. She saw the positioning of the bodies lying side by side as a possible psychological statement by the offender: a perverse dichotomy displaying the couple lying in their marital bed after the horrific violence which took place. 'This image may have been borne out of fantasy, which on that night became a reality,' she said. 'The deaths and appearances at the scene have hallmarks of crime scene staging,' she wrote. 'This appears to be a double murder, disguised as a murder-suicide.'

Stephanie Davies' observations raised significant doubts about the proposed sequence of events offered to the coroner by the police in 1996. Taking into account the inconsistencies, the blood patterning, the items left at the scene and the injuries inflicted on the victims, Davies offered an alternative sequence. It began with the offender planning to commit the crime, possibly someone with knowledge of their euthanasia beliefs, which would provide the perfect cover for murder. The offender gained non-forceful entry into the property, then threatened the couple with the hammers and knife. Howard complied with the demands of the attacker and wrote a suicide note, and the note found at the top of the stairs, while under duress. The notes were laid out in the bedroom.

They were given some alcohol to drink, then Howard was smothered using the plastic bag, possibly with a hand clamped over his mouth, causing injuries to his lips. Once suffocated, he was lifted and placed on the bed, propping him up awkwardly on the headboard and trapping his hand underneath him. Bea tried to escape but was dragged back, causing cuts to her knees. She was attacked with a hammer in the bedroom, causing blood to spatter on the outside of Howard's plastic bag. The hammer was put down and the knife was driven into Bea's forehead. The offender covered her face with a pillow, then washed his hands and the hammer in the sink, getting rid of valuable evidence. As a final act of humiliation, he tugged up Bea's nightie, exposing her genitalia to those who would find her body, making his escape using the backdoor of the house.

'This author cannot concur with the original conclusion of murder-suicide,' Davies wrote. 'The features identified and described above are consistent with double murder. The offender has staged/altered the scene in order to misdirect the police investigation and divert the police away from them.'

13

The Review: Wards

The police investigation into the killings of the Wards in 1999 took a different approach to the inquiry into the Ainsworths, a point well recognised by Stephanie Davies during her review of the case. 'Initially it was very difficult to add anything further to this case because it was an extremely detailed police investigation, and the depth of the inquest file is admirable,' wrote Cheshire Police's senior coroner's officer in her confidential report. 'This case was initially treated as a double murder hence the high level of scrutiny. Expert input was sought from a variety of sources, including extensive forensic testing and offender profiling. Evidence of third party could not be ascertained, so the only hypothesis available to both the police and the coroner was that of murder-suicide.'

Davies' reason for reviewing the case was mainly the remarkable similarities to the Ainsworths' case three years earlier. The coroner's file on the Wards supplied a wealth of information about the couple and the police investigation. There were bundles of witness statements. Post-mortem reports. Detectives' reports. NCF reports. Forensic and toxicology reports. Davies noted there was no documented history of mental illness or marital issues between the couple. Owing to previous break-ins, Donald was apparently 'obsessive' about security in his home. 'They had installed a top-of-the-range alarm system which was routinely turned off at the same time every morning when they woke and set when they either went out or retired to bed,' she wrote. 'Both had sustained violent injuries and the deaths were initially treated as a double murder due to what appeared to be defence wounds on Mr Ward's hands. They were last seen alive on Monday, 22 November, and there were no concerns in relation to their demeanour at that time, although Mr Ward may have been worried about his health recently.'

She began with an analysis of the crime scene photographs. 'The photographs show Mr Ward lying on the left-hand side of the bed, and Mrs Ward on the right,' she wrote. 'Due to the blood at the scene it is clear that both deaths occurred on the bed. They are both wearing their nightwear and there is evidence of a broken pot on the bed. Mr Ward had sustained a deep incised wound to his neck, and there is a knife protruding from his chest. Mrs Ward had sustained head and neck injuries, and a pillow is partially covering her face.' The report shows three stark colour photographs of the couple, their bed drenched in blood, lying in postures almost identical to the final positions of the Ainsworths.

Davies said the images showed evidence of Auriel being 'tucked' into bed, which can be a sign of 'undoing' by the assailant, which is the action of trying to 'undo' the crime against the victim by attempting to make them more 'comfortable' after the act. 'In addition, a bloodied pillow has been placed partially over her face, after she was tucked in,' Davies said. Again, she saw the act of putting the pillow on Auriel's face as a sign of 'depersonalisation'. 'However, as just the part of her face that is facing the exit is covered, it is more likely than not the offender did this to avoid the victim "seeing" him leave,' she wrote. In another stark parallel to Bea Ainsworth, Davies saw that when the bedding was lifted off, Auriel's white crumpled nightdress is 'seen to have folded up, exposing her pubic area'.

The pillow on Donald's side of the bed also concerned her. 'The image shows what appear to be stab marks in the pillow,' she wrote. 'This is strongly indicative of a fight or a struggle against an assailant trying to stab Mr Ward. There is nothing to suggest that Mrs Ward had initially been on that side of the bed (as that was not her usual side of the bed according to the items at the bed-side),' she said. 'Indentations of this nature are not typical at suicide scenes.'

Next, her review dealt with her bloodstain pattern analysis of Donald and his final resting position. 'Whilst there is little in the way of blood impact spatter decipherable in the scene photos (due to the large quantities of blood that has exsanguinated from both Mr and Mrs Ward), a lot can still be interpreted from the remaining blood patterns.' She adds: 'The images show a significant amount of deposited blood, amongst the stab indentations in the pillow. In the top centre of the pillow are blood splash patterns. These were most likely a direct result of when Mr Ward's throat was cut – indicating his approximate position (and that of the knife when it was extracted), at that time.'

She noted the concerns of the NCF officers before her, who had been confused by the lack of an explanation for the blood on Donald's face, meaning his body had either been moved after his death, or an object had been removed from his face, by persons unknown. 'The blood transfer pattern in this image shows Mr Ward's face had been embedded in a bloodied fabric item for a period of time, most likely the pillow underneath him,' she found.

> This must have happened when he collapsed into his pillow after his throat was cut. Of note, the report from Mr Ward's GP confirms he was taking a blood thinner, aspirin. This can increase the rate of blood loss, hence reaching death even quicker. The post-mortem report showed that his jugular vein was cut. Whilst this does not spurt blood as fast as the carotid artery, there would have still been extensive blood loss within a very short period of time.

Davies assessed that when Donald's throat was cut, he must have been lying face down in the pillow for a period of time 'whilst the wound haemorrhaged into the pillow, thus soaking his face'.

He was likely to have been in this position while his wife started to bleed, causing her blood to soak into his pyjamas. This was shown by the patches of blood which had soaked into part of Donald's pyjama top and the lower part of his right trouser leg around the knee and shin areas. The blood was not associated with any injuries on his body, which meant the clothing must have been in direct contact with another blood source. The blood on Donald's right knee belonged to Auriel. To develop patterns of blood of this nature, he would have needed to be in contact with the blood source for a period of time to enable the blood to soak into the clothing. Except, by now, Donald's throat was cut, meaning death in seconds. So how was he found with a knife in his heart staring up at the ceiling? Davies believed this to be possible evidence of Donald's body being moved after he was dead.

Davies looked at the bloodstain patterns around Auriel's body. Her body, hair and bedsheets were damp with water. It was hard to ascertain from the photographs if the blood or water was on Auriel's neck and body first, Davies said. The water had presumably come from the ceramic hot-water bottle, when it broke into different shards. But the photographs of Auriel in bed showed a distinct lack of blood on the neck itself, which suggested the water must have been splashed onto Auriel after she bled from the neck area. 'Even if her neck was stabbed after death, there would still be some blood emanating from these wounds,' she wrote. 'This photograph also shows that her head appears to have been moved after she bled out onto the pillow.'

Moving on from the blood pattern analysis, Davies examined the marks and wounds on Donald's body. There was the deep incised wound to Donald's right palm, stretching from the base of his palm directly upwards, falling short of the base of his first finger. There was also a deep cut between the thumb and first finger on his right hand, as well as injuries to the top of his hand, and marks and bruises on the back of his arm and his inner forearm. She could see why the inquiry team had treated it as a double murder. The wounds looked like defence wounds caused by a sharp knife – perhaps, Davies thought, because that's what they were.

'The pictures above show incised wounds to Donald's hands and arms,' she wrote. 'It was deduced that these [wounds] were caused by a broken shard of ceramic pot when he attacked his wife. However, there are numerous "defence" wounds, so they could equally have been defence injuries against an offender with a sharp knife. The areas that have been injured are consistent with those seen in knife defence injuries.' There was also an injury to Donald's mouth, similar to what she had seen with Howard Ainsworth, which she thought was 'indicative' of an assault.

One of the issues the NCF analysts had with the theory that Donald was the killer was the method he had used to take his life. Was it possible for a 73-year-old grandfather to have inflicted such an extreme level of violence upon himself? Was the method proposed by the police even feasible? 'The pictures above show both sides of Mr Ward's neck,' Davies wrote. 'Note there is no evidence of superficial or hesitation wounds, that are typically seen in sharp-force suicides. The large wound appears to be going from left to right direction, and the smaller wound appears to have gone from right to left (due to the observed tailing of the wound).'

After Donald had cut his throat, the police proposed, he had stabbed himself in the heart. 'Like with the neck injuries, there are no hesitation or superficial wounds seen in the chest areas, which would typically be seen in suicides,' Davies said. 'These marks are common when a suicide victim is gathering the courage to inflict a wound upon themselves. Often, they will try a few tentative attempts first in order to test what would be required to carry out the final act.'

Davies was also concerned about the lack of blood flow coming from the stab wound. 'Considering the knife pierced the heart, there is still little blood flow coming from the wound,' she said. 'If this injury was done post-mortem, it is likely there would be some venous blood flow (Aggrawal, 2014). It really is questionable if Mr Ward was physically able to stab himself in the heart, given the severe injuries to his neck — which would have caused quick death in any event.'

Donald's injuries did not end there. He had a wide gash on his wrist which, again, had little blood coming from the cut. He also had puncture-like wounds to his groin. 'Again, the lack of blood coming from the wounds [to the groin] look like they were done post-mortem,' she wrote. 'Of note, injuries to this area are never seen in sharp-force suicides. This is a site generally chosen by IV drug users.'

Her report considered the marks and wounds on Auriel's body. She found defence wounds on Auriel's hand. One of her little fingers was purple. 'The photograph shows a blunt force injury to Mrs Ward's little finger, where the weapon appears to have had a smaller surface area to the ceramic bottle,' she said, and went on to wonder 'if this could have been made by another weapon, such as a hammer. It could have been done in an attempt to make the couple comply with instructions.'

Auriel had cuts on her right hand where a sharp weapon had sliced her fingers and the spaces between her fingers. While the cuts could have been caused by the broken pot pieces, they were also consistent with the blade of a knife and were similar to the possible defence wounds shown on Donald's hand, Davies said. Auriel's left hand was black and blue. 'This image shows extensive defence injuries — most likely as a result of defending her head against a blunt instrument. This shows she was conscious when she sustained blunt-force injuries to her head.'

The injuries to her head could have been caused by the

ceramic hot-water bottle, causing a number of lacerations on her head, Davies found. But one of the marks on her head was rounded and almost like a puncture wound. 'The photograph below shows a mark that appears to have been caused by a different weapon, such as a hammer,' she wrote. Davies also saw signs of manual strangulation, due to the presence of bruising and fingernail abrasions around Auriel's neck. 'This image appears to look like pressure abrasion patterns, consistent with a ligature having been present at some point (like an offender was stood behind her at the time),' she said.

As on Donald's body, she found evidence of wounds on Auriel's neck which, owing to the lack of blood deposits, appeared to have been carried out after she died. 'These superficial wounds were either done as part of the MO (i.e. ensuring DNA was transferred to the broken pot fragments, or to disguise earlier marks on the neck), *or* as part of signature behaviour (such as post-mortem mutilation).'

Davies knew it was rare for a victim to inflict more than one severe fatal injury upon themselves. The injury to Donald's neck had been more than sufficient to end his life. 'It is highly unlikely he was still alive when the knife was stabbed into his heart,' she wrote. 'This strongly suggests his body was moved and re-positioned after his death.'

Davies offered an alternative scenario to the police's explanation of events. The offender, she thought, may have been known to the Wards and let into the house. Auriel was injured or asphyxiated in order to get Donald to comply with the attacker's demands. Donald was attacked and sustained a wound to his hand. He was forced to get items from the kitchen and made to walk back upstairs. Back in the bedroom, the attacker tried to stab Donald a number of times, making marks in his pillow. Donald's throat was cut, and he lay with his face embedded in the pillow where he bled out.

Auriel sustained a number of blunt-force injuries to the head, probably from the ceramic water bottle and perhaps a hammer, too. She tried to defend herself and injured her hands. She was strangled and repeatedly stabbed in the neck. Her blood soaked into Donald's pyjamas and onto his right foot. Donald was turned over in the bed to face upwards and then stabbed directly in the heart. The offender then added some stab wounds to Donald's groin, and slashed his wrists to make it look like suicide. Water was thrown onto Auriel, diluting some of the blood and washing blood from her neck. The offender pulled up her nightdress and tucked her into bed, placing broken pieces of ceramic pot around her, before covering her face with a pillow.

'The offender knew this couple,' she said. 'He knew about their alarm system and knew what time the alarm would be turned off. Most likely he was let in by the victims, as he was not at that time perceived as a threat by them.'

Davies saw Auriel as the focus of the murder, just like Bea before her. She believed a fight had likely broken out between the attacker and Donald. 'This will be why Mr Ward sustained more violent injuries than required to complete his death,' she wrote. 'Superficial injuries have been made to his wrist and groin, most likely done post-mortem, to appear like they were self-inflicted,' she said. 'The offender may have added these wounds in, perhaps due to the couple refusing to write out suicide notes.'

She found Auriel had sustained 'far more injuries than what

was necessary to cause her death (overkill)'. 'There is signature behaviour evidence with her nightdress folded up, and her face partially covered with the pillow. The superficial injuries to Mrs Ward's neck are either paraphilic behaviour, or MO behaviour to mislead police.'

Davies concluded her review of the Wards' case by saying she could not concur with the original findings by the police of murder-suicide. 'The features identified and described above are consistent with double murder,' she wrote. 'Whilst it is not as obvious as in the last case, the offender still appears to have attempted to stage/alter the scene in order to mis-direct the police investigation, and to divert the police away from them.'

Davies and Hurst found the 1996 and 1999 killings suspicious in their own right, but when the two cases were compared, it merely strengthened their conclusions. Both cases occurred in Wilmslow, either side of the town centre, and a relatively short distance from one another (less than two miles). Both couples were found lying side by side in their marital bed. They were dressed in their nightwear, the male on the left, female on the right.

Both females sustained blunt force injuries to their heads, as well as penetrative stabbing injuries. Time was taken on each female, who appeared the focus of considerable anger. The two women's nightdresses were yanked up to expose their pubic area. Their left hands were positioned in 'almost identical posi-tions', to expose their wedding rings. Their faces were either covered or partially covered with pillows. The bodies of both males 'were rearranged or moved after their death'. There was handwritten evidence at both scenes, either in the form of 'suicide' notes or next-of-kin contact details.

There was no history of domestic violence or psychiatric illness in either couple. Both couples were in reasonably good health, according to their GPs. The actions taken by the men were completely out of character and regarded as 'inexplicable' by the coroners who dealt with each case. Likewise, the police inquiries never uncovered any 'trigger' or reason why the men might have carried out such brutal and humiliating murders on their partners. She concluded in her report that a single offender was likely responsible for both double murders. 'Due to the signs of signature behaviour being evident at both scenes, this means there is a real risk of further similar cases taking place due to the offender's requirement to satisfy intrinsic psychological, paraphilic and fantasy needs,' she wrote.

Stephanie Davies' concerns were such that she decided to widen her search beyond her jurisdiction in the county of Cheshire. 'Due to what appeared to be signs of signature behaviour at both scenes [in Wilmslow] the realisation was made that there could be other similar cases across the country,' she said.

The Davies Review highlighted three more cases of murder-suicides involving elderly couples in the north-west of England which she believed would be worthy of closer inspection by their respective police forces: two in Greater Manchester in 2000 and 2008, and a third case in Cumbria in 2011. As a note of caution, Davies stressed in her report that she did not have access to the coroner's files for the further three cases and was highlighting them simply owing to their apparent similarities to the Wilmslow killings.

She conducted research to identify murder-suicide cases in

married couples which had occurred since 2000. She focused on retired couples over the age of sixty who were found dead at the same time. Cases where the murderer took their own life at a later date were discounted. Many police forces were unable to search back further than a few years owing to the limitations in searching through archived paper files, as well as the problems faced by different IT systems.

Davies found that between January 2000 and September 2019 there were just thirty-nine elderly couples in the UK who had died from murder-suicide. In ten of the cases, both the male and the female had died from asphyxiation, the most common cause of death. Other methods included death by shooting (five couples) and death from sharp-force injuries (four couples). Three of the women were killed using a combination of asphyxiation and blunt-force trauma in cases where the man died from asphyxiation only. Davies was particularly interested in cases where the woman had died from blunt-force trauma and sharp-force trauma, and the man had died from sharp-force injuries and/or asphyxiation. There were only three couples which met the 'Wilmslow killings' criteria. They all occurred in the north-west of England – two of them in Greater Manchester, a few miles away from Wilmslow.

I4

Death in Didsbury

It was love at first sight when Michael and Violet Higgins met in a Manchester dance hall in 1968. There was an instant connection between the two, despite the seventeen-year age gap, with Michael the younger of the pair. He had been born in Carrick-on-Shannon, a small town on the banks of the River Shannon, Ireland's longest river, which grew historically from the spot where the Shannon could be forded. In summer, the boardwalk along the pretty marina would be full of tourists out for an evening stroll, the sun breaking across the marshes, after a meal in one of the local pubs.

Violet had grown up across the border in County Tyrone, Northern Ireland. She had worked as a police constable, serving in Yorkshire before transferring to Manchester. She would spend another nine years in the police in Manchester while married to Michael. Michael worked as a security guard with a building firm. They never had children but were close to their family.

Michael's brother, Daniel, would often remark how much Michael idolised his wife. She had nursed him through cancer and other illnesses, and after he went through the trauma of being diagnosed with Parkinson's disease she was there for him emotionally, as well as caring for his basic physical needs, which became an increasingly demanding task as time went on. He had come to depend on her. In the months leading up to their deaths, Michael was frail. His movements had slowed down and his muscles were rigid. He struggled with his posture and balance, and often couldn't hold a cup in his hand without spilling its contents on the carpet. He developed a slur down one side of his face, as if he had suffered a stroke. Some days even tending to his L-shaped garden had become a laborious and seemingly insurmountable task.

In the aftermath of the shock of the diagnosis, Violet had been there for him. But in February 2000, the cracks were starting to show, as Violet struggled with being a full-time carer. Michael talked to his sister-in-law about the state of his marriage. He said Violet was planning to leave him; that she was thinking about putting him in a nursing home which could provide 24-hour care. Michael had visited a solicitor to get legal advice about a possible divorce. It was the last thing he wanted to do, but he wanted to know where he would stand in the event of a break-up. Then tragedy struck.

The family had been struggling to contact the couple for a few days, and eventually decided to call the police. On 21 February 2000, PC Paul Weir forced his way into their house in Didsbury, south Manchester, an area made famous by the ITV drama *Cold Feet*. Weir was twenty-five at the time. He had been in the police just two years but had already shown an ability and maturity beyond his years, and was tipped by senior officers to rise quickly through the ranks of Greater Manchester Police. 'He was one of those people you look at,' his superior during his initial probation period, Inspector Peter Henson, would say of him, 'and think, "He's something special," and I firmly believe he was destined for high rank.'

Violet was seventy-six when she died. Michael was fifty-nine. Initially it was reported that Violet had suffered serious head injuries and Michael had stab wounds to his neck and body. In similar manner to the Wards' case, after the post-mortem examinations police continued to tell the public they were treating the deaths as 'suspicious'. Detective Superintendent John Kelly, who led the investigation, said there were no signs of a break-in, no valuables had been stolen and there was no sign of a struggle.

Neighbours said the couple rarely went out. Violet suffered from arthritis, and Michael's advanced Parkinson's disease prevented him from going very far. 'It is a terrible tragedy,' Charlie Dillon, one of Michael's childhood friends, told a newspaper at the time. 'They were very quiet. They used to go out to the pub for a drink, but they stopped doing that recently.' Naisen Berraies, a sixteen-year-old who lived opposite, told reporters: 'I thought of them as my grandparents.' The neighbours said children would play football against the wooden fence which lined the boundary of their garden, using it as a goalpost, but the couple were very tolerant and never moved the children on. To the outside world they were a normal happy couple. Michael was gentle and non-violent – a little meek, even. His condition had made him a rather vulnerable character.

Their bodies were found in a terrible state. Michael had died from a stab wound to the throat and a wire coat hanger being twisted around his neck. His body was discovered in the spare bedroom. There were pills scattered about on the nearby bathroom floor. Violet's body was found by PC Weir in the marital bed with the duvet pulled up. She was wearing a nightdress with no knickers. Her face and head had been beaten beyond recognition by a rolling pin. There were stab wounds around her neck from a pair of scissors.

Manchester's detectives realised Cheshire Police had dealt with a similar event in Wilmslow two months earlier and decided to liaise with their counterparts in the neighbouring force to discuss any similarities between the Higgins' case and what had happened to Donald and Auriel Ward. There were clear comparisons to be made. The graphic violence inflicted on the woman. A couple described as devoted to one another with no history of domestic violence. Both victims found in their nightwear. The female sustaining the highest level of violence.

Police scaled down the murder inquiry after a lack of third-party evidence in the house pointed to Michael being the killer. Police said he killed Violet after she threatened to put him in a care home. Shortly before they died, Michael had told his brother Daniel that Violet was thinking about returning to her family in Northern Ireland. She was struggling to cope with his condition. Police thought he had battered her to death because he couldn't stand the thought of being without her. He would rather see her murdered than lose her and end up in a nursing home all alone.

In March 2001, the Manchester coroner Leonard Gorodkin recorded that Violet's death had been the result of an unlawful killing, while Michael had taken his own life. 'It was a very sad end to many years of apparent happy marriage,' said Gorodkin, an experienced coroner who had sat on many high-profile inquests including the British Airtours disaster in 1985 when Flight 28M caught fire before take-off at Manchester Airport, killing fifty-five, and the deaths of twenty-four Britons at the Waco siege in Texas in 1993.

The Higgins case, however, puzzled him greatly. 'I don't know what led to them falling out,' Gorodkin said, 'but the terrible violence that took place was completely out of character with Mr Higgins.' He said that, despite some evidence that Violet was considering a return to Northern Ireland, it remained 'unclear' to him why Michael had decided to carry out the murder suicide.

Likewise, Michael's brother was also mystified. 'It was a great shock,' Daniel told the inquest. 'I never thought of my brother as being capable of hurting anyone.' A violent murder using a rolling pin and a pair of scissors would have required a strength and dexterity which Daniel thought was far beyond the capabilities of his brother considering his advanced Parkinson's. He doubted that Michael had the dexterity required to stab himself in the throat and twist a coat hanger around his neck. Michael struggled to make and hold a cup of tea in the morning, never mind commit a murder-suicide.

Davies asked the same questions in her report. 'Mr Higgins had a history of Parkinson's disease,' she wrote. 'Did he have the strength, co-ordination and dexterity to carry out: i) the sustained and violent assault on his wife; ii) the twisting of a wire coat hanger around his neck after he had stabbed himself in the throat?'

Michael's and Violet's killings had a huge emotional toll, not just on their family but on the police officers who worked on the investigation. The promising young police officer, PC Paul Weir, who first discovered their bodies and carried out an initial assessment of the crime scene, would never forget the horrific violence he saw in Didsbury that day. In the weeks following the incident, he became quiet and withdrawn. He would continue to talk about Michael and Violet Higgins with his colleagues at Elizabeth Slinger Road station in Withington, a suburb of south Manchester. He told them the case had 'imprinted itself on him'. He wasn't able to shake it off.

Seven months later, his fiancée, Stephanie Percival, aged twenty, arrived at their home in Audenshaw, Manchester, to find it locked. She called a relative who gained access to their house and found Weir's body, slumped next to his computer with a small amount of heroin and a syringe in his arm. There was no evidence that he was involved in the drugs scene or had ever done drugs before in his life. His blood was found to contain barely a quarter of the heroin usually found in the bodies of habitual users who suffer fatal overdoses. The small amount of heroin he had used in a one-off experiment proved to be fatal. Speaking at his funeral, Percival spoke of Weir's inner turmoil after visiting the Higgins' house. 'The murder haunted him,' she said. 'I was worried about him after he went in that house.' She had been engaged to Weir for just two days before the overdose. The coroner recorded a verdict of death by misadventure.

For Davies, a potential pattern was beginning to emerge of rare murder-suicides of married elderly couples in a tight geographical area of north Cheshire and south Manchester. She did not have access to the full police or coroner's file for the Higgins case, which meant she had to be careful in her conclusions. 'The combined methods of sharp-force injury to the throat, the pills thrown on the floor and the twisting of the coat hanger around the neck all in combination strikes [sic] as a very rare and unusual suicide method,' she wrote. 'These method(s) and signs of suicide could therefore be indicative of exaggeration at the scene i.e. where an offender tries to make it obvious to the police that the death was due to suicide, rather than a (disguised) murder.'

Davies found a second Manchester case which fitted the pattern of murder suicides. Kenneth and Eileen Martin, aged seventy-seven and seventy-six, lived around ten miles away from Michael and Violet Higgins, in Davyhulme. On 10 November 2008, police were called to their house at 6.05 p.m. after they were found dead in their garage by their daughter, Elaine Tong, and her husband, Dennis Tong. It was the day before their fifty-fifth wedding anniversary. One of the neighbours had seen Kenneth out in the garden the day before. There had been nothing unusual about his manner or demeanour. The family released a statement to the media. 'Today would have been their fifty-fifth wedding anniversary,' it read. 'They were a very devoted couple and the family cannot comprehend what has happened. At this moment we are all in deep shock and would like to be left alone to grieve in peace.'

The inquest heard that Kenneth had hung himself because he could no longer handle looking after his wife. Kenneth had suffered several strokes, diabetes and prostate cancer. He had cared for his wife for the last five years since she had been diagnosed with dementia. He had told his family he was struggling to cope and warned them he would not leave her behind 'as a burden'. Police said he had battered Eileen's head using a blunt instrument before cutting her neck and wrists. After that, Kenneth had apparently hanged himself from the garage doorway.

Elaine, his daughter, told the inquest her father was a 'proud man' who had refused the help of social services in providing care for his wife. He had become depressed and was unable to walk but was also refusing to use a wheelchair. Kenneth wanted his children to inherit his money rather than spend it on their care. He had watched in despair as Eileen's vascular dementia got steadily worse. She would forget who people were and spent hours sitting in a chair staring into space, appearing neither happy nor sad. She had escaped the house several times during the night and had to be locked in for her own safety. 'She just kept getting worse and worse,' Elaine said. 'It drove my dad mad. He used to say, "When it is my time to go it will be her time because I am not leaving her behind as a burden."' She warned her father that he could not 'play God with Mum's life'. She thought his off-the-cuff remarks were simply attention-seeking during one of his low periods.

The night before they died, Kenneth had broken down in tears and admitted to Elaine that he could no longer cope. Elaine tried to reassure her father, telling him that it would be all right, she would visit every single day, and they would get through it together. He had seemed calmer after their chat. But police said that later that day Kenneth had taken his wife into their garage and locked the door, killing her before hanging himself. A suicide note was found. It made for a compelling case of murder-suicide. The coroner commented that Kenneth had a 'misguided belief that others could not or should not cope with his wife'. Afterwards, Elaine bore no anger or bitterness towards her father. 'My mum was a lovely person and my dad was just an old man struggling with life,' she said.

Davies found their deaths had some parallels with the 1996, 1999 and 2000 cases, which is why the case received a mention in her report. The violent injuries inflicted upon Eileen did not appear consistent with a mercy killing. Smothering by using a pillow, or asphyxiation using a hand clamped over the mouth and nose, would be a far more common way of carrying out such a murder. Kenneth's method of killing himself was also suspicious. It was unusual to inflict sharp-force injury to the neck and then die from asphyxiation owing to self-suspension. 'As before, case linkage cannot be made at this stage without reviewing the crime scene photographs or the file itself,' she wrote. Although there were similarities with the Wilmslow cases, the Manchester murder-suicides had evidence of 'significant life events' or 'life triggers' which might go some way to explain the circumstances of the deaths.

The fifth and final murder-suicide mentioned in the Davies Review also featured a 'significant life event' which might explain the deaths of Stanley and Peggie Wilson. Stanley, aged ninety-two when he died, was said to have murdered his 89-year-old wife in their home in Kendal, Cumbria, before taking his own life. Stanley was a retired quarryman who had worked in an abattoir as a younger man. His son Graham knew him as a 'lovely' man, but someone with a temper which could go off with a 'bang'. Peggie had worked as a teacher in Liverpool before returning to live in Cumbria in 1962.

Stanley and Peggie had met while on holiday in Malta. They had both been widowed. Stanley was seventy when they first met, while Peggie was in her late sixties. Neither of them had expected to find love again. They got married in a quiet ceremony at Kendal Register Office — they didn't want to make a fuss, not at their age. They just felt lucky to have some company in their retirement. Their combined families were large and comprised three sons, four grandchildren and three great-grandchildren. They maintained an active social life and were regulars at their local community centre. Stanley enjoyed bowling with his friends, while Peggie took part in activities such as Scrabble, painting and needlework. As far as anybody knew, there had never been any violence or rows between the couple. One worker for Age UK, who used to visit them, would later tell their inquest: 'They were very loving towards each other. She loved him, and he loved her.'

They lived a life of marital harmony and were enjoying their lives in the picturesque market town. But that sense of harmony came to an abrupt end when Stanley reached his nineties. He started to suffer paranoid delusions about Peggie trying to alter his will for her family's financial benefit. His health was causing him a great deal of distress. His poor eyesight meant he had to give up driving, and shortly after Christmas 2011 he had an operation at St Paul's Eye Unit inside the Royal Liverpool University Hospital for a detached retina.

Many family members highlighted the operation as a turning point in Stanley's decline. It was the end of his independent life. One day, Peggie's daughter Sandra Smith, who was living in Leeds, got a phone call from her mother. Peggie said Stanley was accusing her of trying to poison his meals. He was even refusing to drink a cup of tea if she brewed it, believing it might be laced with poison. Such behaviour was completely out of character for Stanley, and it was getting worse. He told one of the neighbours he 'felt trapped' and that Peggie was 'trying to murder him'.

Then one afternoon, Stanley walked out of the front door of their house on Mint Dale Street, located just outside the centre of Kendal, and didn't come back. Peggie was out of her mind with worry. Stanley was eventually discovered on a nearby street by their postman, Neil Taylor. Stanley was in clear distress, waving around a piece of paper in his hand. He urged Taylor to read it. Stanley had written a note which accused Peggie of mixing up his medication so it would affect his memory and make him more likely to change his will.

The incident forced Stanley's family to take action. They couldn't allow him to simply walk out of the front door in such confusion and get lost wandering the streets of Kendal, making baseless accusations about Peggie. He clearly wasn't well. An appointment was arranged with Stanley's GP. The doctor diagnosed Stanley with 'acute confusion' and said he should be admitted to hospital until he showed signs of improvement.

On 25 January 2011, Stanley was admitted to the Royal Lancaster Infirmary and provided with round-the-clock care by the nursing staff on Ward 5. He was medicated with anti-psychotic drugs and regularly assessed by a team of clinicians. At one point he accused the nursing staff on the ward of trying to poison him. He repeated his fears about his family trying to murder him in order to benefit from his will. He was in hospital for three weeks, where he was thought to have made a successful recovery. The hospital staff believed he had vastly improved from his previous paranoid state through a mixture of medication and therapy sessions.

Stanley appeared to have reached a turning point. Peggie was able to visit him on the ward and Stanley was seen kissing and being affectionate towards her. He seemed to be genuinely hurt and distressed at the upset he had caused, and accepted that what he had said about Peggie and his son trying to poison him had been completely wrong, and was extremely remorseful.

He even told the nurses he was excited about returning home. 'If you're ever passing by, make sure you pop in for a cup of tea with me and Peggie,' he told several staff members. 'You're always welcome.' The hospital took the decision to discharge Stanley on 17 February. It was a decision that would later be closely scrutinised and heavily criticised by the coroner.

The day after his release, Stanley's son Graham, who worked as a wagon driver, and his wife, Barbara, visited the house on Mint Dale at 7.49 p.m. after they had failed to raise anybody on the telephone. They entered the house using their spare key. They found no signs of forced entry into the property. Barbara walked into the front bedroom. Her heart froze. It was covered in blood. Stanley and Peggie were lying on the floor.

Peggie had been punched and strangled. There were injuries to her face and head from blunt-impact trauma and she had defence wounds on her hands. She had been stabbed a number of times in the neck with a knife taken from the knife block in the pantry of the kitchen. Police believed Stanley may have taken the knife to bed with him the night before in preparation for the attack, or perhaps took the knife in the mistaken belief he would need it to defend himself from Peggie. Stanley himself died due to a number of knife wounds to his neck. Most of the wounds were superficial, suggestive of tentative first attempts at self-injury as he worked himself up to a deliberate act of self-destruction.

Graham and Barbara never suspected any foul play. Indeed, Graham thought his father's old job in an abattoir would have made him more 'comfortable' around knives and blood. He blamed the hospital for releasing him too early and thought his father should never have been discharged into the community to go back and live with Peggie. By doing so, he felt, the hospital and the authorities had let his family down. Peggie was frail and would have been unable to hold him back for long.

The hospital's decision to discharge Stanley was criticised by Ian Smith, the coroner for south Cumbria, who recorded that Peggie had been unlawfully killed, while Stanley had taken his own life suffering from 'acute mental illness'. After hearing testimony at the inquest from a number of hospital staff involved in his treatment, he said that Stanley's condition on Ward 5 had 'fluctuated very considerably day-to-day, hour-to-hour . . . the medical staff thought he had recovered, and he had not . . . The fluctuation was not fully recognised and acted upon. There was an assumption it would get better and if Mr Wilson said he was okay and wanted to go home, then he was better – when he clearly wasn't.'

Stanley's death appeared to be a classic case of an elderly person in great need whose care had fallen through the cracks in the system between various teams of social workers, mental health workers and hospital medics. 'The truth is no one was really in charge of the process,' the coroner told the inquest. 'He was effectively discharged by default.'

Davies took the five murder-suicide cases and examined the victimology of the couples, victimology being the branch of criminology that examines the relationship between the victim and the offender, and the reasons why the victim may have been targeted. The obvious common factor between all five cases was they were all elderly, retired couples living in their own homes. They were all described by their family as being 'devoted' married couples with no history of domestic violence. Four of the couples were found in their main bedrooms.

The only couple discovered outside of their bedroom were the Martins, who were found dead in the garage.

When an offender is selecting a victim, whatever the crime, the vulnerability of that person is often a factor they will consider. The most vulnerable groups tend to be children, elderly people or young women. Generally speaking, the older a person, the more vulnerable they will become, owing to a number of physical and mental factors. The youngest of the five men by far was Michael Higgins, who was fifty-nine when he died; however, he was also one of the most vulnerable, suffering from advanced Parkinson's disease. The oldest was Stanley Wilson, aged ninety-two. Hospital staff said he could still wash and dress himself on the ward but could be 'quite slow'. Out of the five women, the youngest was Auriel Ward, who was sixty-eight and had some problems with her hips but was otherwise in decent health, while the oldest was Peggie Wilson, aged eighty-nine when she died, and described by family as 'frail'.

Davies believed the five couples, should the Wilmslow cases be linked to the other three cases, would not have been victims of opportunity, but were likely to have been targeted due to their specific vulnerabilities. 'Planned murders are notoriously hard to solve compared to impulse homicides,' she wrote. 'This is due to the lack of forensic evidence left behind, the lack of eyewitnesses and the offender being able to choose when to carry out the crime.'

After her review of the available evidence, Davies felt certain the Wilmslow cases were double murders and recommended the three further cases were worth a closer look due to their obvious parallels. She considered the sort of offender who would have committed such crimes a serious danger to society who had to be identified and captured. 'This offender would have meticulously planned every detail of these murders,' she wrote.

> He ensured he was forensically aware to leave as little evidence as possible. The offender will have spent a period of time after the deaths setting the scene and admiring his handiwork. There also appears to be an element of arrogance and ego expressed at these scenes. He may have even taken a photograph, or a 'souvenir' from the scene so he always has a reminder of the events that took place.

She saw him as somebody who enjoyed humiliating his victims, particularly the females, by posing their bodies and exposing their private parts. He would inflict wounds after death, known as 'post-mortem mutilation', and he would do so because of a psychological or fantasy-based need. She saw the offender for the Wilmslow killings as displaying an 'anger-retaliatory signature (Keppel and Birnes, 1998) (Turvey B., 2012)'. This was someone with an explosive personality and a short fuse.

He would choose adult females from his own age group or older because they were representative of a dominant female in his life whom he perceived to be the root cause of his problems. During the act of murder, the victim would be transformed to become the source of all his frustrations. He might also be triggered to commit a murder due to a recent event associated with the dominant female in his life. For example, a row with that person could mean he went out to kill a person in their image. He would target only victims who represented this female and would be unlikely to attack at random. He might take time before choosing the right female who met his criteria.

There was evidence of overkill at the crime scenes through blunt-force and sharp-force trauma along with manual strangulation. Such an offender, postulated Davies, used 'weapons of opportunity' found at the scene but also brought weapons with him. 'He does not see himself as committing a crime,' Davies said. 'He sees it as avenging the actions of this dominant female and creating justice and balance.' His attitude after the murder had taken place would be: 'She deserved what was coming.'

'Once the anger eases and the realisation sinks in as to what he has done, he has to move the victim's face away from him,' she wrote. 'He cannot leave the scene with her facing him or seeing him leave. He will attempt to ensure her eyes cannot see him and turn her head or cover her face. This then reduces the feelings that this dominant female is still judging and disapproving of him.' She believed the offender may have known the couples in some way and had perhaps befriended them. He would have learnt the detail of their daily routines. He only targeted elderly people, probably because they were physically weaker, which would allow him to dominate and control their actions in their own homes leading up to the murders.

Davies then issued a chilling prediction in her report. The sort of person she believed capable of such crimes would never stop. Not unless somebody stopped him first. 'This individual will not stop killing until someone or something stops him,' she warned the police. 'It is likely he has had paraphilic fantasies for the majority of his life. The acts of dominating the victims, carrying out the murders and fooling the police are addictive to him. He will have meticulously planned each murder, ensured he left no forensic evidence and followed the cases in the media. With each killing he will have gained more and more confidence and egocentricity.'

The internal police systems showed a number of boxes of evidence were being stored in police archives relating to the Ainsworths' and the Wards' cases. Davies did not have access to these separate archives in writing her report, which were based entirely on the coroner's records, and largely heard in evidence during the original inquests. The police archives showed at least one box in storage for the Ainsworths' case and eight boxes in storage containing evidence relating to the Wards. She recommended that a full independent review be carried out, along with a forensic review of the existing evidence, including the murder weapons.

Forensic techniques are now available to the police which did not exist in 1996 and 1999. Scientific breakthroughs such as DNA17 mean that forensic testing can now examine seventeen areas of DNA. Small particles of fragmented or 'partial' DNA can be traced back to their owner, a technique which has only become available to police forces in the last six years, while hair strands of just 2mm in length can now be used to build DNA profiles – forensic methods which would have seemed like science fiction to the detectives working homicide cases in the '90s.

Davies concluded her report with a personal declaration, one which came from the heart. 'It has been an extremely difficult decision to submit this report to the relevant authority,' she wrote.

The decision was made due to the concern that there is an outstanding offender, who could still be offending, and who needs to be brought to justice. This is to also support those affected families who still believe their fathers/grandfathers/ uncles/brothers have violently killed and degraded their wives. And finally, this is to ensure that the truth comes out for those deceased victims themselves.

The findings of the report were supported by Christine Hurst, who submitted a witness statement to be read in conjunction with the Davies Review.

Davies handed her report to the police in September 2018. She waited for feedback from the major crimes team. None came. She received vague promises from senior detectives that they would 'get around to reading it' when they had the chance. Davies had the distinct feeling that the contents were too problematic for the police. Her report had been tucked away in a drawer somewhere and apparently forgotten about.

But Davies wasn't willing to let it go. She had seen evidence over the course of her review of a dangerous offender at large who had been missed by two investigation teams. She had started this project out of curiosity, and because of her PhD research on the subject of equivocal death. Now she regarded it as part of her duty as the police force's senior coroner's officer to get this matter taken seriously by the senior ranks. The next step was to have her report considered by an expert independent of Cheshire Police who could provide her with a neutral opinion of its findings. She wanted to be certain. And she knew just who to ask.

15

Salt Lake City

Anyone walking into Stephanie Davies' office in Warrington Town Hall in early 2019 would have seen a piece of card pinned to the wall with the word **AMERICA!** scribbled on in big capital letters. It was a reminder that her flights were booked, and she would soon be travelling to Salt Lake City in Utah to meet with Arthur Steve Chancellor, one of the most respected criminal investigators in the United States. She had arranged to attend one of his advanced homicide training courses.

While they were there, he had informally agreed to take a look at the Wilmslow cases. As one of very few experts in the world who specialised in crime scene staging, Chancellor was the perfect person to provide a second opinion. Davies wanted to know what he would make of the deaths of Howard and Bea Ainsworth, and Donald and Auriel Ward. She maxed out her credit cards and saddled herself with thousands of pounds of debt to book her flights and hotels.

British police forces will often send senior and specialist officers over to the United States to learn advanced techniques from the FBI and the other various law enforcement agencies. Simon Barraclough, one of the North-West's most senior counterterrorism detectives, was sent to train with the FBI in post-blast investigation, which helped him when he later led the inquiry into the Manchester Arena bomb attack. The difference with Barraclough was that Greater Manchester Police had footed the bill, while Davies was paying out of her own pocket to meet one of the world's leading experts in his field.

Chancellor, known to most by his middle name 'Steve', had enjoyed a long and successful career in the US Army. A Californian by birth, he had gone straight into the army as a military policeman in 1973, and in 1981 joined the army's criminal investigations division (CID) as a special agent, to investigate felony crimes on military bases, or crimes involving soldiers who had got themselves into trouble with the law off base. In 1995 he was part of the team which investigated the Oklahoma City bombing, when a US army veteran, Timothy McVeigh, driven by anti-government beliefs and a desire to spark an American revolution, parked a truck packed with explosives outside a federal office building in Oklahoma City, killing 168 people, including a number of children, in one of the worst terror atrocities seen in the US. Chancellor was deployed as a representative of the US Department of Defense liaising with FBI investigators to establish the circumstances around the terrorist attack.

During his long career Chancellor had investigated every type of murder and suicide imaginable. Four years before the Oklahoma bombing, he was based in Fort Lewis, Washington, where he led on a quadruple homicide, a traumatic case and the most graphic and bloody crime scene he had ever encountered. Two drug dealers had entered a house on an army base belonging to a soldier and his family and executed him and his three young children.

The dealers, who belonged to a local gang called the 'Blood', believed that the soldier was providing the police with information about the gang and its drugs-supply network. They entered his home and used knives to hack the soldier into pieces. Afterwards they slit the throats of the children, three boys aged seven, five and one. Their mother was a soldier herself, based in Korea at the time. She tried to contact the family and couldn't get hold of them. She called a neighbour, who went inside the house and found the bodies. Chancellor walked into the property to find a dead child in the hallway, another stuffed into a closet, and a third who had had his throat slit in the living room before being dragged and thrown into a bedroom and left to die. It took Chancellor two weeks to catch the drug dealers, who had fled to Los Angeles.

In 2001, Chancellor retired from the US Army and took a job as a senior crime analyst at the Mississippi State Crime Lab examining and assessing violent crime scenes. Three years later he transferred to the Mississippi Bureau of Investigation (MBI) and was the first director of the MBI cold case unit, responsible for assisting police agencies across the state with unresolved homicides. He is the co-author of *Crime Scene Staging: Investigating Suspect Misdirection of the Crime Scene* and a co-author of *Death Investigations: The Second Edition*, regarded as some of the most respected works in the field of crime scene analysis in the US.

The first book was written as a practical reference manual for detectives, crime scene investigators and prosecutors on how to recognise a staged crime scene and how this sort of offender behaviour can be used as evidence in subsequent trials, drawing on the authors' thirty years of experience of investigating homicide. Chancellor's career later saw him develop training courses for the Mississippi State Police Academy on basic and advanced crime scenes, death investigations and adult sex crimes. A graduate of the FBI National Academy and fellow of the American Academy of Forensic Science, he now runs training courses with Grant Graham, a forensics expert and the co-author of *Crime Scene Staging*.

Chancellor had got to know Grant Graham when they worked together at the Mississippi Crime Lab. Graham had previously worked for US Air Force Security Police before being appointed a member of the FBI's Kosovo War Crimes Task Force. Like Chancellor, his job at the Crime Lab was to examine violent crime scenes throughout the state and provide detectives with his assessment of the evidence.

Graham's background was in forensics. He had been an instructor in forensics at the Mississippi Law Enforcement Officers Training Academy and was a member of the Fayetteville State University Forensic Science Program Advisory Committee. He is currently the forensic manager for Fayetteville Police Department and a leading expert in the field of bloodstain pattern analysis. Together, Chancellor and Graham run their own consultancy called Second Look, which carries out training for detectives, prosecutors and even FBI agents looking to hone their investigative skills and sharpen their reading of crime scenes. They teach detectives how to spot staged crime scenes and show them how to look for the red-flag indicators.

On Tuesday, 12 March 2019, Stephanie Davies flew from Heathrow to Salt Lake City. It was the start of the spring season, and her plane touched down on a runway sprinkled with feathery snow. She had come prepared for the cold and had wrapped up warm in her winter clothes. At the Hilton Garden Inn a message was waiting for her. *Stef: We are heading over to the police department for 7.15 tomorrow if you care to join us. Steve Chancellor.*

Davies spent a restless night thinking about her report into the Wilmslow killings and the frustrations of it sitting in a drawer in the office of the major incident team, completely ignored. It was exactly the same response as Christine Hurst had encountered. The police thought they knew better. They always did. She was a female civilian investigator. What did she know? What right did she have to question the police's findings? How could she have spotted something they had missed?

By now, every aspect of the Wilmslow cases felt seared into her brain. She felt confident in her findings but at the same time nervous. Would Chancellor and Graham agree with her findings? Or had she missed something obvious? Was there some flaw in her rationale which might undermine her report? That was why she was here. A second opinion. She wanted to know what they thought, even if it contradicted her report.

In the morning she walked into the hotel's spacious dining room to find Chancellor and Graham waiting for her. Chancellor, dressed in suit and tie, was a big guy, over six feet tall, with a wide frame, a side-parting of brown hair and glasses. The sort of person who was comfortable around people, made them feel at ease with a folksy charm that belied a sharp investigative mind. Davies warmed to him immediately. Graham was taller and thinner, more serious in his manner. Colleagues would sometimes joke, 'Don't *ever* argue forensics with Grant Graham,' such was his knowledge of the subject.

Over breakfast Davies told them her background, but knew the first morning of the course was not the right time to lay the case before them, so waited for a more appropriate moment when the two men were relaxed and could give her their full concentration.

At Sandy Police Station, where the course was being held, the room was full of detectives from law enforcement agencies in New Hampshire, Montana, Idaho and Utah. Chancellor stood up at the front and started his talk. Offenders were smarter than ever before, he said. They have learnt how to avoid leaving evidence, and how to adapt crime scenes in order to throw investigators off the scent. One of the key factors in spotting when a murder was staged to look like a suicide, he went on, was when the offender had gone 'too far' in making it obvious to police that the victim had taken their own life. Pills scattered about like confetti. Weapons placed in hands. Bodies moved around and left in awkward positions. To Davies it all sounded eerily familiar.

The class broke at around 4 p.m. and Davies arranged to meet Chancellor and Graham an hour later for dinner in the hotel to go through the Wilmslow case files. In the private lounge Chancellor and Graham ordered a beer. Davies decided on a glass of water: she wanted to stay completely focused. When she could see she had their full attention, she started. 'My old boss has never been happy with these cases,' she began. 'She was the coroner's officer who worked on both of these murder-suicides at the time. They happened not far from each other in a small town in England. I was hoping to get your views.'

She had not shown them her report or told them any of its findings. She had made that decision on the flight over: she wanted to see if they came to the same conclusions on their own without any influence from her. Chancellor and Graham examined the crime scene photographs for the Ainsworths' case first.

Straight away, Chancellor saw the lack of blood on Howard Ainsworth as a problem. 'I'd expect to see a lot more blood on his pyjamas.' Chancellor frowned. He knew from experience that the human head is extremely vascular. In cases like this, when a laceration starts to bleed, repeated blows of a hammer on top of that wound should cause blood to be thrown all over the attacker. Chancellor had seen it countless times before. But Howard was practically spotless. It made absolutely no sense. Graham thought the same. It didn't look right.

Chancellor noted that a suicide letter had been found in the bedroom. But then, a note like that was not always irrefutable evidence: he had once dealt with a case where no fewer than three suicide notes had been found at the crime scene. In March 1991 Corporal Chris Davis, based at Fort Lewis in Washington State, had murdered his wife, Dorothy, who was thirty-three at the time. Davis had shot her in the temple with a pistol and placed the gun into her hand, then laid out three different suicide notes he found hidden in her journal. He left a bottle of pills beside her and returned to a local bar, arranging his alibi with some friends.

The coroner found the gun in her hand and the suicide notes to be compelling pieces of evidence and ruled that she had committed suicide. But friends and family were sceptical, particularly Dorothy's sister. Then a witness from the bar came forward to say Davis had actually been missing for twenty minutes and had come back into the bar without his jacket. That same jacket was found at the crime scene. Further forensic tests were then carried out on the envelopes containing the suicide notes to see who had licked and sealed them. The DNA results came back as a perfect match for Chris Davis.

Chancellor saw the presence of a suicide note in Howard and Bea Ainsworth's bedroom as being important, and clearly some of its contents had been written contemporaneously. But could the note have been written by Howard under duress? Or could it be a letter which Howard had not acted upon, which the killer then discovered and used as the cover for murder? Or could the handwriting expert simply have been mistaken?

Chancellor and Graham asked to see the photographs from the Wards' case. Their initial observation was that the bedding had a curious lack of bloody prints considering the severe wound on Donald's hand. The bedding and blankets were pulled up over their bodies – if Donald had pulled up the blankets and 'tucked in' Auriel after the murder, where were the bloody marks? 'There should be more blood on the bedding given how much blood is on Donald's hands,' Chancellor remarked. Again, Graham agreed. 'That's a big red flag for us,' Chancellor said. 'It really jumps out.' Chancellor was also worried about the number of injuries inflicted on Bea Ainsworth and Auriel Ward. They were women in happy marriages. The methods didn't fit.

Chancellor was hooked. He had seen enough in this quick scan of the photographs to know that something wasn't right with those murder-suicides. But he wanted a chance to look into the cases in more detail than was possible over drinks in a hotel lounge. 'You may have a point here,' he said. 'If you like, we could take a closer look for you?'

Davies breathed a deep sigh of relief. There had been so many moments of doubt. Christine Hurst had been so certain they were double murders that perhaps it had clouded her own judgement. Her respect for Hurst's professional opinion might have affected her own neutrality. But Chancellor and Graham had come to the same initial conclusion. The evidence in the bedrooms didn't stack up to a murder-suicide. She agreed to work with Chancellor, and in the coming months he would apply his vast level of experience and knowledge to the cases, uncovering startling new evidence which even Davies had not considered.

Steve Chancellor began working on his own report shortly after Stephanie Davies arrived back in the UK. He had been deeply impressed by Davies and her expertise, particularly in the field of blood spatter analysis, in which she excelled. She understood the principles of what should be present in each crime scene and, perhaps even more importantly for an investigator, what was not present but should be. In Chancellor's experience investigating homicides for the military and the police, detectives without an advanced level of training often do not come to the realisation that the crime scene has been staged unless it is pointed out to them. People tend to believe what they see – even experienced detectives. Like others before him, Chancellor was surprised by the violence on show. This was not commonly found in murder-suicides involving elderly couples.

His report started with the Ainsworths. At the top of the document he gave a frank assessment of the findings he was about to outline. 'I have received the main points of the police investigation pertaining to the deaths of Mr and Mrs Ainsworth and I would not concur with their findings of murder-suicide,' he said.

> I believe this is more consistent with a double murder. Clearly Mrs Ainsworth was murdered, but based on my review of the material, I would not accept Mr Ainsworth as the murderer. I believe he was a second murder victim. There are several indicators that I note are consistent with staging, wherein the offender has altered the scene for the purpose of misdirecting the police investigation.

Chancellor saw that the Ainsworths were 'dressed as prepared for bed'. 'They were both found in the marital bed where the actual murders took place,' he wrote. Howard had been described by those who knew him as a 'private person' making it unlikely he would have chosen to murder his wife and kill himself in his nightclothes in their own bed.

> My concern is that if Mr Ainsworth came to the point of murdering his wife, would he choose the marital bed for such a violent act? Further, that he would murder his wife while she is dressed in nightclothes, which, as noted in the scene photographs, caused her nightgown to ride up above her pubic area, which certainly would have been degrading or embarrassing. The question is – would Mr Ainsworth have been concerned with how his wife was found?

Chancellor acknowledged Howard's belief in euthanasia and the concept of 'death with dignity'. 'Mr Ainsworth certainly subscribed to the concept of euthanasia and indicated that he planned to end their lives when it became too much for them,' he said.

> The concept of euthanasia is a more planned death and one using a combination of alcohol and drugs and other means to slip off into sleep and thus ending their lives peacefully. This makes Mrs Ainsworth's violent death the most inconsistent factor for this being a case of murder-suicide. Mr Ainsworth's own comment [in the suicide letter] that he was ready but thought he might have to throttle Mrs Ainsworth in order to cause her death — throttling is of course strangulation. Clearly this method that he was considering prior to the offence was not attempted.

He saw that Howard's head was leaning unnaturally against the headboard, his left arm trapped underneath his body. 'Looking at his final resting place in the bed I observed that Mr Ainsworth's head was not resting on the pillow as if he were going to sleep but appears to be leaning unnaturally against the headboard . . . In my opinion this is consistent with him being placed into the bed by an offender after he was already dead.'

Like Davies, Chancellor saw a great deal of emotion in the offender who attacked Bea, consistent with rage. He believed Bea was the target, with the greater anger, energy and effort expended on her, rather than Howard. There were two main objects used in the assault: the hammer that caused the blunt-force injuries to Bea's head, and the kitchen knife impaling her head. Chancellor said the offender would at some point have had to stop hitting her with the hammer to pick up the knife and continue the assault, making it a particularly vicious and sadistic attack. The third weapon found at the scene – the hammer resting on the cabinet – was out of place with the bedroom and 'consistent with an offender bringing it to the death scene', Chancellor said.

The main murder weapon was the hammer found in the sink, which had been washed. 'It is unclear why this was necessary unless it was an effort to remove any potential forensic evidence left by the offender,' he said. 'This effort is a distinct break in the event, meaning that Mrs Ainsworth and Mr Ainsworth were murdered and then the offender had to stop, take the hammer to the sink and wash it off, and then rinse the sink out.'

One of the most disturbing elements of the crime scene was the idea that Bea's attacker had pulled up her nightdress to expose her to the people who would find her. Chancellor was in no doubt that it had been consciously yanked up by the person who killed her. 'The initial CS [crime scene] photos of the Ainsworths in bed appears [*sic*] that the left side of her nightgown has been pulled up to intentionally expose her pubic area,' Chancellor said. 'This does not appear to be the result of movement by the victim as it is gathered at the left hip consistent with someone pulling it up slightly.'

Then there was the curious lack of impact blood spatter on Howard's clothing or his hands – something which had concerned Davies, and Chancellor had spotted at first glance in the hotel lounge. Blunt-force trauma injuries, especially to the head, are known to produce blood spatter. Indeed, there was blood sprayed all over the headboard attached to the bed – just not on Howard. The second, third and fourth blows to Bea's head with a hammer would have resulted in blood spatter being thrown over her attacker. 'I am concerned forensically by the fact that Mr Ainsworth has very little impact blood spatter on his clothing or hands,' Chancellor wrote in his report.

> BFT [blunt force trauma] injuries are known to produce spatter as noted on the headboard. Yet the small number of stains found on Mr Ainsworth's clothing are totally inconsistent with being the perpetrator of this homicide. I would expect the front and the cuffs of the long sleeves of his pyjamas to have stains at a minimum. I am not sure of any position Mr Ainsworth could put himself into if he caused the injuries to Mrs Ainsworth that he could have avoided receiving any bloodstains during the assault. There were a few stains on his pyjamas, but I believe this is more consistent with him being in bed or nearby at the time the injuries were inflicted on Mrs Ainsworth.

Chancellor turned his attention to the suicide note itself. The bloodstain on the note was consistent with the letter being present in the room at the time of the assault, or an object which had later dripped blood onto the note. But the contents of the letter made very little sense to Chancellor. 'The contents of the note outlined medical issues that were causing Mr Ainsworth to consider the double suicide, but the note is in direct conflict with what Dr Redhead [Bea's GP] stated – that Mrs Ainsworth had a viral infection and was getting better and should be okay in a few days,' he said. 'The most important aspect of this diagnosis is that it was not a serious health issue.

I find it hard to believe that this was not communicated to Mr Ainsworth, or Mr Ainsworth decided that she didn't want to wait until she got better.'

The pathologist who examined Howard's body at the time had been mystified by the presence of two bruises either side of Howard's upper lip. The post-mortem found the injuries were not consistent with the plastic bag suicide method that Howard had used to supposedly take his own life. 'Mr Ainsworth has what appears to be injuries to his lip,' Chancellor wrote. 'I believe this might be the result of being suffocated as these are the injuries that are caused by that type of event. No direct evidence of this, but it would be an explanation.'

Chancellor was also concerned by the findings in the toxicology report which showed a very small amount of alcohol in Howard and Bea's urine. 'To me this is consistent with both consuming some amount of alcoholic beverage some time prior to their death,' he said.

Neither of the levels [of alcohol found in Bea or Howard] were consistent with intoxication. I find this important because if she had consumed alcohol, then why not take the pills in order to complete the double suicide? If this was a planned event certainly Mr Ainsworth could have placed the pills into her beverage if needed, then once she was asleep could have easily and non-violently placed a plastic bag over her head and ended her life. Then he could have done the same thing to himself. An autopsy showed Mrs Ainsworth had 190ml of food material in her stomach, meaning that shortly before her death she had consumed some food. This is inconsistent to me that food was prepared and eaten, and an alcoholic beverage was consumed but then Mr Ainsworth violently assaulted her.

Chancellor doubted Howard was capable of behaving in such a violent manner against his wife. The means he used were inconsistent with his euthanasia beliefs. 'Mrs Ainsworth's life was not ended with dignity, it was ended with violence, and she was left in an embarrassing or degrading position. This is so out of character, I cannot concur with the initial police finding [of murder-suicide],' Chancellor said. 'I do see signs of staging being present, as noted in the inconsistencies, and I would have looked at this as an example of offender efforts to misdirect a police investigation . . . I would not concur with their [Cheshire Police's] findings of murder suicide. I believe this is more consistent with a double murder.'

Little about the case made sense to Chancellor. Howard could have suffocated Bea with a pillow over her head. She would have died in a relatively short period of time in a far more dignified fashion. The killings didn't fit any known facts or information about Howard and Bea, and the presence of a letter could raise any number of possibilities.

Chancellor believed the Wards presented an even stronger case for being a double murder. In his professional opinion it was inconceivable that Donald had inflicted that number of injuries upon himself. Chancellor had seen everything in his career. People who had stabbed themselves up to a hundred times. One case he investigated involved a man who had killed himself using a chainsaw. But like the National Crime Faculty analysts, Christine Hurst and Stephanie Davies before him, Chancellor had doubts about a person being capable of cutting the jugular vein in their neck, then still having the strength or the mental awareness to be able to stab themselves in the heart with a kitchen knife. This was the stuff of Japanese samurai movies, not a 73-year-old grandfather from Wilmslow who suffered from mild anxieties about his health.

'Observed the stab wound to Mr Ward's chest,' Chancellor said.

I do not see any hesitation marks or shallow cuts near the stab wound which are common in cases of suicide with a knife. Typically, there are several of these shallow cuts as the victim stabs themselves several times until they work up the courage or determination to make a final plunge of the knife. These are absent. The other wounds in the lower positions of his body are inconsistent with hesitation wounds. Also, they are not in locations on the body I would consider consistent with self-inflicted stab wounds. Also, I did not detect any actual bleeding from the other stab wounds to Mr Ward, indicative that these may be post-mortem injuries. I question the ability for Mr Ward to stab himself so deeply in the chest after suffering the large wound to the neck. The injuries to the neck are so severe I just can't imagine that he then would stab himself so deeply.

In Chancellor's view, Donald's neck injuries would result in a loss of consciousness in seconds, followed by rapid death. Donald would be able to do very little as blood squirted from his neck. Chancellor, a graduate of the FBI and a special investigator for the US Army based out of Fort Bragg for many years, who still investigates cold cases on behalf of a number of US law enforcement agencies, thought it was extraordinary Cheshire Police believed it was even possible.

In fact, he had issues with a number of Cheshire Police's findings with regards to the evidence in the house. The police had decided the telephone cable was loose from its socket because Donald wanted to disable the telephone. 'I am not sure why this was important if he intended to murder his wife and end his own life,' Chancellor wrote. 'This action appears to be a premeditated event as it most likely occurred before Mrs Ward was assaulted. It is more likely the phone was disabled by an offender, prior to the murders to perhaps prevent the Wards from calling for assistance. But this is inconsistent behaviour and unnecessary if this was a murder suicide.'

Chancellor did, however, see the ceramic hot-water bottle as a curious object to use as a murder weapon. 'This appears to be something that was handy rather than an object purposely sought to use as a murder weapon,' he said. He had seen such weapons used in the past during domestic violence situations that had escalated into physical assaults. However, there was no history of domestic violence between the Wards. 'I am suspicious that a domestic violence incident resulting in a violent murder took place at this age and time of their marriage without a prior history of violence,' he said.

Chancellor saw signs that Auriel's neck injuries had been inflicted post-mortem. 'If these injuries were inflicted perimortem – as part of the violent assault – I would have expected these injuries to have bled,' he said. 'But looking at the photos of Mrs Ward in situ at the scene I see no signs of bleeding from any of the shallow incised wounds. I believe these injuries were inflicted some time after death.' Her nightgown, like Bea's, was pulled up to expose her pubic area. Again, Chancellor's opinion was that it was not the result of Auriel's movement in the bed, but rather a deliberate lifting up of her nightclothes, since there was a similar gathering of the material above the hips consistent with the gown being pulled up intentionally.

One of the most important inconsistencies for Chancellor was the lack of bloody handprints on the bedcovers. He had said as much to Davies and Graham over drinks at the hotel in Sandy. Now, after spending some time reviewing the evidence, he was certain that the missing blood marks from Donald's hands created a serious contradiction to the police's murder-suicide hypothesis.

'The bed covers have been pulled up to Mrs Ward and the lower position of Mr Ward post-mortem as they cover up Mr Ward's lower legs which are bloodstained,' he said.

The bed covers also cover what appears to be a partial bloody handprint. To me this is one of the biggest inconsistencies within the scene. Clearly at some time during the event Mr Ward's legs came into contact with some blood source (most likely Mrs Ward) which was transferred onto the pyjama legs. But then the bedcovers (blanket) was placed over his lower legs covering up this stain. But if the covers were pulled up or over his lower legs following Mrs Ward's assault, I would have expected to see signs of transfer of blood from his hands onto the blankets – especially if his own hand was injured during the assault. But I saw no blood consistent with this action.

Chancellor added: 'Also covered up by the blankets appears to be a blood handprint next to Mr Ward's legs. Again, this shows that the covers at one point were lowered to allow the handprint or bloodstain to be placed upon the bottom sheet – the covers were then pulled up or moved to cover Mr Ward's lower legs and the bloodstain.'

Chancellor, like Davies, noticed a number of marks or 'defects' in the pillow next to Donald on the bed which were consistent with stab wounds. Why would Donald have been stabbing his own pillow? There were no signs Auriel had been on that side of the bed during the attack. 'To me this is inconsistent with a suicide event,' he said.

He saw no motive for murder or suicide in any of the documentation or evidence surrounding the Wards' case. Cheshire Police believed Donald had 'settled his affairs' shortly before the killings. But Chancellor simply saw evidence of long- and short-term plans being carried out. The work on the driveway. Paying the newspaper bill in advance. Auriel's hair appointment. Birthday celebrations with the family. Medical appointments. Arrangements for Christmas day with the family. Arrangements to babysit their grandchildren. There was plenty of interaction with relatives and friends in the weeks preceding their deaths and no obvious signs of depression or any significant life event which may explain the trigger for a murder-suicide. Again, for these reasons, Chancellor thought the Wards' case was more consistent with a double murder.

In isolation, each of the Wilmslow killings presented serious concerns for Chancellor. But together, they made a compelling case. 'Most murder-suicide events are the result of an escalating domestic violence situation or are the result of a specific pre-cipitating event,' he wrote.

> By precipitating event I refer to some action on the part of one partner that causes the other partner to become so enraged they murder the offending partner and then take their own life. I did not see any indication within either investigation or through any victimology assessment that would be consistent with domestic violence being an overriding motive for a murder. I also did not see any precipitating event in either case which may have led to the murder of either victim. I am also concerned with the extreme amount of violence inflicted on the women in both events and the exposing of the pubic area of both victims. I would interpret these injuries as expressions of anger and rage by the offender upon the female victim.

Howard had been left practically untouched. Donald's injuries were 'extensive', but Chancellor believed those injuries to be consistent with self-defence efforts as he fought back. 'Although I cannot state 100 per cent for certain that the same offender was involved in both incidents . . . I would be looking at the same offender involved in both cases as a very real possibility.'

Chancellor saw the parallels. The murders took place in the victim's house. The events occurred within the master bedroom or marital bed. There was a combination of blunt- or sharp-force injuries inflicted on the female. The female's clothing was adjusted in order to expose her pubic area. The female received more injuries than the male. Some of the weapons used originated in their house. The doors to the houses were left open. And there was no precipitating event leading up to the incidents. He noted the two murder-suicide cases in Manchester had displayed many of the same characteristics. In Chancellor's view, Cheshire Police had a duty to re-open and investigate the killings from scratch, because it was likely a serial killer had been operating undetected in the north-west of England since the mid-'90s.

16

'Stop Rattling My Fucking Cage!'

The turn of the twentieth century would mark an end to detective work as an undocumented art form in favour of its computerised modern-day equivalent. One of the catalysts for this evolution was the publication of the Macpherson report in February 1999. Two years earlier, Jack Straw, then Home Secretary, had asked Sir William Macpherson, a retired high court judge, to inquire into the matters arising from the death of Stephen Lawrence in order to identify the lessons which needed to be learnt for the investigation and prosecution of racially motivated crimes.

Lawrence was eighteen when he was murdered in south-east London in 1993 by a gang of five or six white thugs. He had been running to catch a bus with his friend Duwayne Brooks in the suburb of Eltham when he was set upon, one of the attackers calling out 'What, what, nigger?' Lawrence was stabbed to a depth of about five inches on both sides of the front of his body to the chest and arm. Both stab wounds severed axillary arteries. Blood was literally pumping out of his body as he ran down the road to escape his attackers. He managed to get 130 yards before collapsing, something which amazed the pathologist, Dr Shepherd, who remarked that it was a testimony to Lawrence's physical fitness that he was able to run so far.

It became one of the most high-profile murder cases the UK had ever seen, partly because nobody was brought to justice following the murder. The *Daily Mail* newspaper conducted an award-winning campaign examining the murder in great detail. After Lawrence's inquest in February 1997, the *Mail* ran a front page which showed a picture gallery of five men with the headline: MURDERERS. Underneath the now famous headline was a message: 'The *Mail* accuses these men of killing. If we are wrong, let them sue us.'

The Macpherson report looked into the Met's investigation of the Lawrence murder and examined every detail of what had occurred from the moment of Lawrence's death to the public hearings at Hannibal House in south London. At the point when the report was published, nobody had been convicted of Lawrence's murder, an affront to both the Lawrence family and the community at large. It was only due to the groundbreaking cold case forensics work carried out by Dr Angela Gallop that in 2012 two of the group of attackers, Gary Dobson and David Norris, were convicted of murder.

The Macpherson report found that Lawrence's murder was entirely motivated by racism. But its 389 pages also laid bare the fundamental errors in how Scotland Yard, supposedly the 'gold standard' for detective work in the UK, had gone about investigating a major homicide. The investigation had been marred by a combination of professional incompetence, institutional racism and a failure of leadership by senior officers.

There was found to be an 'astonishing' lack of direction and organisation during the vital first hours after the murder took place, the key 'golden hours' for any police investigation. An almost complete lack of note-taking by officers made the exact reconstruction of those hours almost impossible. There was a lack of properly co-ordinated action and planning and, despite large numbers of police officers available on the night, 'inadequate measures' were taken to use these officers properly. This was due to the failure of direction by senior officers who attended the scene, the report found, each one of them appearing to think that tasks were being carried out satisfactorily by somebody else. The Lawrence murder utterly exposed the chaotic nature of how major homicide investigations were being run by the UK's largest force.

After the publication of the Macpherson report came a lesser-known study by Martin Innes, a professor at Cardiff University and part of the Police Science Institute. The study was called 'Beyond the Macpherson Report: Managing Murder Inquiries in Context' and it looked at the systemic problems that had bedevilled the investigation of murder inquiries in the '90s. Detectives often categorise murders as self-solvers or whodunnits. Self-solvers are easy. They tend to involve people who are known to each other and kill one another in a state of heightened emotion. Stranger murders are more difficult. They account for roughly 30 per cent of all murders in England and Wales.

Innes said the weak point of any murder inquiry was in the first few hours when an organisational framework was in the process of being set up. At the time the UK had no bespoke major incident teams. A detective inspector would be appointed who would then beg, borrow and steal personnel from around the force to set up their inquiry team. Record-keeping was haphazard. There was no requirement for senior officers to record decisions, which made any review of the investigation impossible. Detectives might keep an informal 'day book' for notetaking and for random thoughts about clues, but there was nothing approaching a system of accountability.

Modern-day detectives are required to create a decision log. The time and date of every decision is written down. Part of the aim is to guard detectives against tunnel vision. All too often, detectives would arrive at a crime scene, make a determination on what happened and have tunnel vision until the conclusion of the investigation, with no previous documentation or note-taking which could support how they had arrived at such a conclusion. Police inquiries have also improved how they use HOLMES, the computerised system used to organise the evidence around a major inquiry. During the Lawrence inquiry, detectives were inputting information on a 'first come, first served' basis, rather than evaluating the evidence based on its quality. This meant a huge amount of effort was being placed on inputting information that was irrelevant to the inquiry or its objectives.

Forensics were also going through a period of evolution. Year by year forensics were becoming more important to homicide investigations. In the '90s, criminals were being convicted based on results of 1 in 1,000. During Gary Dobson's trial in 2012 for the murder of Stephen Lawrence, evidence was produced of a blood spot found on his grey bomber jacket, in the weave of its collar, measuring 0.5mm by 0.25mm. The chance of the blood coming from anyone other than Lawrence was 1 in 1,000,000,000 (one in 1 billion).

A number of improvements were made by police forces

across the country following the Macpherson report. Record-keeping began to improve, better training was put in place for senior detectives, rather than the previous 'learning it off your mate' approach to becoming a detective inspector. Policing during the '90s was undergoing an evolution from an imperfect system into one approaching modern-day standards. By the time the Wards' case was being investigated, detective work was starting to transition from an art form into a computer-assisted science.

On a clear sunny day in July 2020, on the doorstep of a terraced cottage somewhere outside Wrexham in Wales, I spoke to John Ainsworth, the son of Howard and Bea Ainsworth, and told him about a confidential report in the possession of the police which said his father was not responsible for murdering his mother back in 1996. He needed to sit down. He dipped inside the dark interior of the house, brought out a stool and put it down in the porch and sat, his legs half in and half out of the door. He was sixty-two and had long left Wilmslow, where he'd grown up. 'I wouldn't want to live in Wilmslow, for fuck's sake,' he muttered. 'Sterile place, now. I remember it as a village.'

He'd been forced to move back to Gravel Lane for a few years at the age of forty-two while he tried to sell his parents' house. Finding a buyer wasn't easy: nobody wants to live in a home where an infamous murder has taken place. John had an interest in journalism: he respected the work of Nicholas Tomalin, the famous *Sunday Times* investigative reporter who had died in 1973 reporting from the Golan Heights. 'You're standing on the shoulders of giants, my friend,' he told me gruffly.

John had strong views about the police and how they dealt with the death of his parents ('complete f**kwits'). He talked about his frustrations at the lack of urgency the police had shown when investigating their deaths, and claimed a key witness was only interviewed after he'd badgered them to do so. But he never questioned the eventual findings of their inquiries – that his parents had died in a murder-suicide carried out by his father.

He remembered the moment his life altered course. It was the weekend Oasis played Maine Road in Manchester, a fact which had always stuck in John's head. 'I don't think there's any other salient date other than Oasis at Maine Road, which is why I lobbed it at you,' he said. Nineteen ninety-six was the height of the Britpop era, when Oasis battled Radiohead and Blur in the charts. It was the year of the Dunblane Massacre, when scout leader Thomas Hamilton walked into a school in Scotland and killed sixteen children, a teacher and himself. Dolly the sheep was born; John Major was prime minister; and Diana, the Princess of Wales, divorced her husband Charles, the Prince of Wales.

John was sleeping in bed when the doorbell of his house in Derby rang out. He checked the clock. It was 2 a.m. on 29 April 1996 – the early hours of Monday morning. He answered the door to find Sergeant Grewal, of Derbyshire Constabulary, standing outside in the dark. John thought it would be the news that his mother-in-law, who had been ill for a while, had finally passed away. Grewal said his mother and father had been found dead at their house in Wilmslow.

There is nothing that can prepare you for news like that. John felt numb. He swapped details with the officer and in a state of shock went back to bed and fell asleep. In the morning he went to work at the charity where he supported recovering addicts in a drug rehabilitation programme. He explained what had happened to his boss, who told him to take some time off work. John rang Wilmslow Police Station and spoke to PC Baguley, who made arrangements for him to be received at the station later that afternoon. John arrived at 2 p.m. with his friend Robert Kershaw. He was met at the station by Detective Inspector Hibbitt, who dispatched two of his detectives – DC MacGill and DS Lowe – to accompany him to Gravel Lane.

He entered his parents' house and checked the rooms to see if anything was missing or out of place. There was nothing. The main bedroom had been scrubbed clean of blood. 'There was one spit of blood I found about five years later,' he said. 'It had been incredibly well cleaned-up.' He went back to Wilmslow Police Station for a debrief with the inquiry team. He was to be spared the process of identifying the bodies in the mortuary. Robin Currie, the undertaker for Albert R. Slack, Bea's former boss, had done the job for him. DC MacGill showed him a sheet of yellow paper on which John's name, address and telephone number were written. John confirmed it was his father's handwriting.

John told the officers the last time he had seen his parents was two weeks before they died. There was no particular reason for the visit. He tried to see them on a monthly basis. John gave the police an alternative story to the assessment by Howard's GP. John considered his father physically sound for a man only six weeks shy of his eightieth birthday, but he had noticed some recent subtle changes in his behaviour. He was lacking his old self-confidence and was more reluctant to travel far from the house. John wondered if his father had developed a rapid and undiagnosed form of dementia.

The last time he saw them, he had visited them at the house. It had been snowing. John had driven through a blizzard to get to Wilmslow from Derby and the alternator on his car had packed up. Howard had tried to help John fix the car – he'd taught John all the car mechanics he knew. But Howard was at a loss how to carry out the repair work. 'I thought at first he was just being a dick,' John said. 'But then I realised it wasn't that.'

He remembered his mother having some troubles with her mobility after recently breaking her leg, which, in his view, might have tipped his father over the edge. She was becoming frailer, despite her mental sharpness. John was well aware of his parents' euthanasia beliefs: he had been told by his father about the suicide pact with his mother. Howard promised they would take their own lives only when deteriorating health had significantly reduced their quality of life. Of the two, John considered his father's belief was probably stronger than his mother's, but his mother was always present when such matters were discussed.

John knew his father to be a complex man. 'Both my parents had awful wars,' he said, shaking his head. '*Shocking* wars.'

Howard was a soldier who had fought in the Burma campaign, a series of battles against the Japanese in the British colony of Burma during the Second World War. The Japanese had occupied Burma knowing it would give them a gateway into India, where they hoped the population might rise against the British Raj. It would also help cut off valuable supplies into China. The fighting between the British and the Japanese was long and bitter: both sides knew they had to wipe out their enemy in order to return home. The soldiers fought in dense jungles, on the banks of the River Chindwin, and the open plains of upper Burma. Howard was one of them.

He was separated from Bea for six years. They remained engaged during the war, but he would come back a different man to the one who left. More serious and circumspect; one who had lost a certain quality of 'lightness'. He never spoke with his family about the fighting, but he had seen many of his friends killed in combat by the Japanese. John believed he had suffered quietly from depression for a number of years, probably driven by his experiences in Burma.

'A lot of that was playing on his mind,' John said. 'I don't have a problem with the logical steps my dad took. I can't say I agree with it. But, you know, there's a logical sequence.' His eye caught sight of a dark hoverfly landing on a plant over my shoulder. He took an interest in nature. Insects. Birds. Same as his father in that respect.

We talked about John's parents and his own life after they died. John built a career as a youth worker. He had a great deal of experience of the police. He was cynical about their methods and didn't trust them. We exchanged numbers and would later have another conversation about his parents and their mysterious deaths. John was intrigued by the idea that his father might be innocent. He wanted to know more. He said his father was not only a member of the Scottish euthanasia society, but also of the Dutch version of EXIT. John thought the Dutch membership appealed to Howard because they were more hard-line than the Scottish group. 'It appealed more to his very strongly held beliefs on euthanasia,' John said. He said his father had a method of suicide on tap. But he recognised his mother's choice for her own death would not have involved being impaled with a large knife.

There was one thing that had always puzzled John. Two years before his parents died, Howard had begun to destroy all the paperwork in the house. 'He went to great lengths to remove anything that could be used to find out anything that he'd been doing, particularly in the last bit,' John said. 'That, I've never understood.'

As a result of the paperwork destruction, John found precious little evidence relating to his parents' lives in their final years. It made John wonder if his father had had help to carry out the euthanasia pact. Another EXIT member, perhaps? 'If there was a third party involved, that's the most likely possibility,' John said. 'My dad's been blathering to somebody in EXIT because it was a bee in his bonnet, and another EXIT supporter has come to the house to give him a hand.'

He thought the police inquiry could have been better. He found out his mother had been seen by her local GP, Dr Claire Redhead, shortly before his parents died. He knew she would be an important witness for the police investigation. According to John, he had had to 'nag' the police to speak to Dr Redhead as a witness. His rather abrasive relationship with the officers on the inquiry had led to some bust-ups. After his trip to Wilmslow to view his parents' house, John returned home to Derby, and went back to work for a short period, before he left his job, feeling unable to continue in the circumstances. While he was still at work, John says, his telephone rang. He picked it up.

'John Ainsworth?'

'Yes?'

'Stop rattling my fucking cage.'

John was convinced the anonymous caller was an officer for Cheshire Police annoyed at him for hassling all the officers to carry out full inquiries into the death of his parents. He was even regarded as a suspect himself, he said, until his mother-in-law provided him with an alibi for being in London that weekend. He had taken his ex-wife Rosemarie to see her mother.

I tracked down Rosemarie to a sheltered housing estate in Droitwich, Worcestershire. The building was made up of small ground-floor apartments where elderly people lived in rooms of peeling wallpaper and mismatching furniture. 'You get all sorts in here,' she told me, her accent carrying notes of east-London twang. 'I can't be doing with the stuck-up ones. You can be as stuck-up as you like, but those sorts have a job keeping it together when they're wetting themselves in front of the staff.'

Rosemarie was seventy-six. She was frail but mentally sharp. Her hair was bone white and frizzy, and she walked with a hunched frame. She had once lived in a sixteenth-century farmhouse with a piano. Her piano was long gone now. In her living room an opera aria was playing softly in the background on Classic FM. 'I'm not university educated, but I'm clever,' she said. 'I've got a very high IQ, hence why I got on well with John, and other people of a certain ilk . . . I've got a mind like a computer – I just can't sodding work one.' She enjoyed watching satirical comedy like *Mock the Week* or *QI*; not the new 'vulgar' sorts of comedy, but comedians who were dry and witty. She got on well with John because of his 'good sense of humour'.

She kept photographs of her former in-laws, Howard and Bea, in a drawer in her apartment. She remembered the weekend they were killed. John had driven her down to London with their two children in order to visit her mother, Mary, who was in poor health. It was one of the last times she saw her. Rosemarie remembers John calling her to say what had happened. 'He phoned me to tell me,' she said. 'My mum said, "You should go back to him and see him." When you hear things like that, it just kind of hits you in the head.'

Rosemarie remembered Howard as being a little overbearing. Like John, she thought that if Bea had resisted euthanasia, Howard might have gone ahead anyway with her murder. She hadn't received a great deal of affection from her in-laws. 'Bea was more affectionate, given the chance,' she said. 'But she was a fussy bugger. Everything had to be in its exact place around the house, and she would call you up on it if it was wrong. Howard was part of all that. "You don't shut the curtains like that, you do it like this,"' Rosemarie said, waggling her finger, doing her Howard impression.

'They never talked about euthanasia and we never raised it. We didn't hang around with them too much – they were a bit stiff and starched for me. I like a bit of a laugh, you see. Mind you, they could have a chuckle, too, now I think about it. I think they saw me and John as being a bit of a comedy duo: John was a bit of a comic. We used to entertain them – we'd always get them laughing in the end, even if they didn't want to at first. They were interested in walking and intelligent and sensible things. I don't think they knew what to make of me and John sometimes.'

Howard was a 'big bloke' and physically strong, even in the

last few years, according to Rosemarie. Bea was 'only little' and had lost some weight the last time she visited her. Rosemarie had always believed that Howard was capable of the murder. That is – until she heard how Bea had been killed. For the last twenty-four years, Rosemarie had been under the impression that her mother-in-law had been strangled. She knew nothing about the murder being carried out with a hammer and a knife. Rosemarie was horrified. 'No,' she said bluntly. 'Absolutely not. There is no way Howard would have ever done that to her. He loved her.'

I visited Gravel Lane in Wilmslow. Many of the neighbours were reluctant to talk about the killings. It was a dark chapter for the street, where the average house sells for more than £600,000. Many living there had arrived too recently to know about what happened in 1996. I spoke briefly to Halton Cummings, who still lived in the same house with his wife, Jacqueline. I told them about the doubts within Cheshire Police that Howard had killed his wife after all.

'Never,' Halton exclaimed. 'I can't believe it.' He had not seen anything suspicious on the weekend of the killings. No prowlers or burglaries. There was one thing he did remember, though. Margaret Farror, the neighbour on the other side, had her bedroom adjoining the Ainsworths' master bedroom to the rear of the buildings. She slept with her dog in that room. 'They heard nothing,' he said. 'Not a peep all night.'

An elderly man with combed-back white hair, who lived opposite the Ainsworths, insisted that Bea had cancer. 'Cancer, she had,' he said. I told him that was not correct: her medical records said she was fit and healthy; there was no mention of cancer. 'They had a pact. If one of them was going, they were both going. She had cancer,' he repeated. 'That's why he did her in.' A second neighbour repeated the same cancer rumour. The story had clearly done the rounds on Gravel Lane.

Robin Currie, the retired local undertaker who had once run Albert R. Slack funeral directors, had worked with Bea for four years before her retirement. From what he had seen, Howard and Bea were just a normal married couple. 'He would turn up at the office sometimes on a Miss Marple-style bicycle – you know, the sort with the little basket on the front,' Currie said, speaking to me over the telephone. 'He was very polite and cheery. He would usually finish work later than her. I think some of his gardening for the council was based around Knutsford, and he would get stuck in traffic on the commute home. On the occasions when he was off work, or finished up early, he would sometimes cycle to our office, or walk, and pick Bea up. They lived just around the corner, across the park.'

According to Currie, Bea had retired early in order to spend more time with Howard, who had already left his job as a parks gardener. She was a big loss for the family-run firm. She had been good at putting people at ease when arranging funerals for their loved ones. Many people she dealt with kept in touch with her long after. Like most people, Currie was stunned when he found out how they had died. His firm had a contract with Wilmslow Police Station at the time – they were one of two funeral directors in the area alerted whenever an unexpected death occurred in the community. Currie had arranged the transfer of the Ainsworths to Macclesfield Hospital mortuary and helped the police to formally identify them. 'You would never have thought that Howard could do something like that,' he said, remembering him as a gentle giant. 'But who knows what goes on behind closed doors?'

17

'They Were 100% Murdered'

Mary Colborn-Roberts was an attractive lady in her sixties with flowing blonde hair straight out of a shampoo commercial. She was the perfect advert for her business, Salon Pampas, a long-established hairdressers on the crossroads between Moor Lane and Cumber Lane in Wilmslow, where the streets are wide and the houses are detached. She took a break from cutting hair to sit with me at one of the swivel stools positioned along a long mirror set into the wall.

The room had the sweet and dry smell of freshly cut hair, and in the background a middle-aged lady was having her hair cut and blow-dried while chatting away to Janet, another of the hairdressers, their conversation punctuated by bursts of laughter. Mary had heard it all in this salon. Money worries. Affairs. Divorces. In the last few months she had heard every theory there was about Covid-19 , including one customer's theory that the Chinese had a deep-seated hatred of old people, so had let loose their own man-made virus to cleanse their population. 'You'd be surprised what people tell me,' Mary said with a raise of her eyebrows, two perfectly plucked arches.

She hadn't just been Auriel Ward's hairdresser. The two had also been close friends. Auriel would come for an appointment every Thursday, and the two would chat for hours. Mary said Auriel would use very little make-up and tended to dress in navy-coloured clothes bought from Marks & Spencer. She wore sensible shoes and was 'no drama queen'; was quietly spoken but had a great sense of humour. She was slightly self-conscious about the 'glide' in her eye. 'She realised people over the counter were just focusing on her eye,' Mary said. 'It was like one of her eyes just had a will of its own.' But she would laugh it off later with friends. 'She didn't have a good head of hair. I remember it being quite fine.'

Mary's close bond with Auriel was recognised with a special mention at the Wards' joint funeral service, held at St Bartholomew's church in Wilmslow, an invitation-only ceremony because of all the media attention. 'Thursday wouldn't be Thursday if she [Auriel] didn't go to Mary's and have her hair done,' one of the sons told the gathering of friends and family, sitting in cold pews in the depths of winter, many still in disbelief.

'She was a lovely woman,' Mary said. 'She talked a lot about her sons and their children. I saw her every single week for years, and she had a good, happy marriage to Donald. She would have told me if it wasn't. They used to go to the Lake District for their wedding anniversary. Sometimes they would go with their family.'

The news of the Wards' death had come as a complete shock to the hairdressers at the salon. 'It's pretty horrific to stab your wife and then stab yourself,' she said. 'It was even more unusual for its time. There are so many violent things on the television now. But you're going back a long time. Things like that didn't happen in Wilmslow. The Wards were very close to a family called the Bells – Mrs Bell – she's dead now. She lived behind them on Manchester Road. She never believed Donald did it. Neither did I.'

Janet finished with her client and joined the conversation. Like Mary, she had also cut Auriel's hair and knew her well. 'There was nothing with Auriel that made me suspect something was going on between her and Donald,' she said. 'The clients can come in and unload on you if they're having problems at home. We've had a fair few people having affairs, telling us they're having an affair, or their husband is having an affair. We never heard anything like that from Auriel.'

Auriel had an appointment scheduled at Salon Pampas that Thursday morning, 25 November 1999. In the past, whenever she had had to cancel an appointment at the last minute, she had always rung up Mary to give her advance warning. For her simply not to show up was unheard of. That Friday morning Auriel was supposed to be meeting her friend, Constance May Boulton. After Mary had phoned Auriel at home and got no reply she had given Constance, whom Auriel was meant to be giving a lift to the airport, a note to post through the letterbox to check she was all right. Detectives had found Mary's card at the house, which is why they had tracked her down and interviewed her along with her husband.

'I remember one of the detectives said, "We'll get to the bottom of this – it's not like it's Wythenshawe,"' Mary said. 'Well, back then, Wythenshawe had quite a bad reputation. I remember my husband saying, "So, do the people in Wythenshawe deserve justice any less than the people of Wilmslow?" They didn't know what to say to that.' Mary claimed the officers had asked her about a tinted hair they had found in the house. 'They asked me about her hair being tinted, because they had found a fibre or a hair in the house that had a tint on it,' Mary said. 'But Auriel never had her hair tinted. She never had any colour in her hair.'

Mary had kept in touch with the Ward family before and after the funeral. One of the three sons had told her they didn't think their father killed their mother. 'They didn't believe it because Donald was a chemist, you see,' Mary said. 'They said he had enough tablets in the house to kill himself, so he didn't have to use a knife. There were a number of things he could have used, and he had the knowledge. It didn't make sense. The way they died wouldn't have been a death of choice for either of them.'

She remembered Donald as being quite small and slightly built. He wore a trilby, and if he you ever walked past him in the street, or met him outside the grocery shop, he would sometimes tip his hat to you. He was quiet and considered, like his wife: 'The sort of person who would probably make an ideal neighbour,' Mary said. 'I can't see him murdering Auriel like that. I really can't see it.'

The Wards' neighbours on Lacey Grove also had their doubts. Roger Bugler, Donald's friend and neighbour who lived two doors down, and is now in his nineties, has staunchly refused for the past twenty years to accept that Donald was the murderer. Roger knew Donald extremely well. They would often spend their afternoons together, having a drink in each other's gardens. Their wives were friendly, which made socialising easy. The men had a lot in common. They were both retired from professional careers: Donald the research chemist, Roger the railways engineer, with an engineering degree from Cambridge University. Roger was adamant: Donald would never have killed his wife. There was just no reason to do it. It simply wasn't in him to inflict that sort of violence upon himself or others.

The Wards' only other neighbour on Lacey Grove, Wendy Smith, the NHS nurse, was slightly more ambivalent towards Donald, but never once suspected he could be a killer. Donald could be quite sweet and romantic with Auriel, Wendy said: he would worry about her talking outside in the cold, and often bring her a coat when she was working in the garden or chatting over the fence to Wendy. But then there were a couple of times, when Wendy and Auriel were having coffee in Hoopers' department store café in town, when Auriel commented that she would like to get back home before Donald returned. It wasn't that Auriel was frightened of Donald – not that – but it did seem that Auriel felt guilty about going out with her friend without inviting Donald. It left Wendy wondering if Donald could be a little controlling.

As the local Neighbourhood Watch organiser, Donald would note down the registration plates of any cars which visited Wendy's house when she was at work, and inform her when she got home. It was overly cautious, but Wendy put it down to him being a bit bored and nosy in his retirement. She never regarded Donald as being any sort of threat to his wife. In fact, she thought, if he *was* going to murder somebody and then himself, it would have been part of his OCD nature to have committed the act more 'tidily', rather than making such a mess of the house.

I was several months into my investigation into the findings of the Davies Review, and being helped by Jonathan Calvert and George Arbuthnott, fellow reporters at the *Sunday Times*. Together we had broken some of the newspaper's biggest stories in recent years, working for the world-famous Insight investigations team, set up by the late Sir Harold Evans and currently led by Calvert, the Insight Editor.

We had helped expose widespread doping in athletics, leading to many Russian athletes being barred from the 2016 summer Olympics; investigated allegations of war crimes by British special forces in Afghanistan; and revealed a Downing Street cover-up in which the news of a Trident missile test misfiring off the US coast had been concealed from Parliament just before a vote on renewing our nuclear deterrent. We had carried out undercover operations to expose sports doping doctors in London and Kenya, and been part of the European Investigation Collaborations group (EIC) which investigated the Football Files, a data project consisting of 18.6 million documents, one of the largest leaks in sports history, uncovering tax avoidance by some of the biggest names in football.

We were eager to speak to a police officer on the inside of the Wilmslow investigations: somebody who could break through the public relations shield erected by the force's press office and provide us with the inside take. We had tried a number of officers, from constables up to senior detectives. One officer told me he had received an email from Cheshire Police. 'They know you're trying to speak to people about the Wilmslow cases,' he said. 'We've been told to keep our mouths shut if you come calling.'

But then one officer did agree. He was nervous. He didn't want to be identified. By the side of a country road in Cheshire, somewhere deep in the countryside, he pulled up his car and got out. It was a remote spot. Nobody would see us talking. He had served in the police for many years doing a variety of different jobs. He had good experiences of working for the force and was loyal to its detectives and senior officers. But he was keen to give me some background.

'We did a lot of forensic work on the Wards' case and found nothing tangible that could put a third person in that house,' he said. 'Does that mean it's impossible somebody else was there? No, of course it doesn't. There might have been. But if there was, we couldn't prove it, which is different to ruling it out altogether. At some point during a large inquiry like that, there has to be an end point. There are all sorts of pressures – pressures on the budget, pressures on the resourcing. More incidents are coming in every day which need to be investigated. That's the reality of policing: you draw a line and look at where you are at that point. What is the most likely conclusion based on the available evidence?

'At the point where we concluded the Wards investigation, the most reasonable explanation was that Donald Ward had murdered Auriel Ward and taken his own life. It was the explanation which best fitted the evidence, in my view, and I was fairly happy with it. But some of our conclusion was based on negatives. We found no solid evidence that a third person was in the house, but we never managed to conclusively rule it out. There was some evidence which could appear to contradict Donald being the killer. But investigations can be like that. Sometimes it's impossible to explain every single detail of what happened. You're always left with a few awkward strands that don't quite fit.'

What about the Ainsworths' case? Was it linked to the

Wards'? The officer took a moment. 'The inquiry team were aware of the Ainsworths' case. It was treated as a historic murder-suicide. There was a theory that Donald might have read about the Ainsworths in the local papers and copied what Howard Ainsworth did, which is why Donald left the door open in the house, the same as Howard. We never found a real reason for Donald doing what he did. I thought he might have had a row and just snapped one morning. In my view, that was the most likely explanation.'

The *Sunday Times*'s own investigations into the Wilmslow killings uncovered no 'trigger events' or 'significant life events' which might explain Howard's and Donald's actions. The Manchester cases did reveal possible trigger events, however, which could go some way to explain, but certainly not justify, the actions of Michael Higgins and Kenneth Martin. Michael Higgins was afraid his wife, Violet, was about to put him into a nursing home and leave him to return to Ireland. Violet was his entire world. He loved her. Some of his close friends said he may have loved her too much. The thought of her leaving him was unthinkable, went the hypothesis, and, in a moment of madness, he killed her and himself, believing it would be better to die than be without her.

The case of Kenneth and Eileen Martin also featured a significant life event. Kenneth was struggling to care for Eileen after bouts of ill health but remained too proud to ask the authorities or his family for help. He took her life and his own, believing, perhaps, in his own mind that he was doing everybody a favour. But despite the obvious possible triggers, there remains some doubt, particularly in relation to the Higgins case due to his physical condition.

After the *Sunday Times* published a series of stories in August 2020 based on the Davies Review, the Higgins family issued a statement which made their position clear. 'We the family of the late Michael Higgins would like to issue a statement on the recent Insight investigation report surrounding the deaths of Michael and Violet Higgins in February 2000,' the statement read. 'We welcome the report as we have always believed that Michael was incapable of committing the acts described in the coroner's report. Michael was suffering from advanced Parkinson's disease and had become very frail. He also suffered from cancer which affected his sight. We knew Michael as a kind, gentle and intelligent man who was devoted to his wife, Violet.'

Stanley and Peggie Wilson's deaths in Cumbria in 2011 also revealed a significant life event in the run-up to their deaths which may explain what happened. The couple were found dead in their home the day after Stanley was released from hospital where he was being treated for acute paranoia, mistakenly believing that Peggie and his son were trying to poison him and change his will. It would be a startling coincidence if the Wilsons had been murdered by a third party the day after he was released from hospital, suffering from such delusions. Or the perfect cover.

Before publishing our investigation, the *Sunday Times* had an expert check over the findings of the Davies Review to provide us with an independent assessment of the evidence. Peter Kirkham, a former detective chief inspector, spent twenty-one years in the Met, spending five years on the Flying Squad dealing with armed robbers, and serving as a homicide SIO for five years. He now works as a policing services consultant and still trains police officers in advanced investigative techniques.

'The report, in my view, raises sufficient serious valid concerns to merit a review of these deaths,' said Kirkham after reading the Davies Review. 'The police should ask an experienced criminal profiler to review this report initially, followed potentially by blood spatter and pathology experts,' he went on. 'This review makes allegations that there may be a serial killer on the loose and provides a large number of reasons for coming to that conclusion. That evidence should now be examined.'

On balance, Kirkham thought it unlikely the Wilmslow deaths were caused by a single person: he had never seen an offender being able to control his victims in such a way before rendering them incapable. But there were a number of elements about the killings which did concern him. 'The first thing that jumped out at me was the knife in Bea's head, and in the second case, it was the knife in Donald's chest,' Kirkham said. 'They rang alarm bells. It's a significantly higher level of violence than what I would expect to see, and quite extreme violence for elderly couples like this.' Another cause for concern was the hammer being washed down in the sink in the Ainsworths' upstairs bathroom. 'Again, that would rate quite highly on the sliding scale of suspicion,' he said. 'On a scale of one to ten, one being the lowest level of suspicion, I would regard the washed hammer in the sink as an eight out of ten.'

Nazir Afzal, the chief prosecutor for the North-West between 2011 and 2015, and best known for bringing child sex gangs operating in Rochdale to justice, was also concerned by the findings of the Davies Review. He was all too familiar with the way that police forces with stretched resources could operate. 'The police can often have tunnel vision, and very commonly they will not look for anything outside of a fixation on a particular outcome – often the easiest one,' he said. 'The concerns raised in this report need to be taken very seriously as we could potentially have a serial killer in our midst. There needs to be a proper review of these cases and others which carry similar hallmarks.'

It was now 21 August 2020, two days before the publication of a front-page story in the *Sunday Times* which would reveal that the senior coroner's officer for Cheshire had written a report concluding a serial killer had been operating in the North-West since the 1990s. Jonathan, George and I were engaged in some frank conversations about the evidence of each case in the weeks leading up to publication – conference calls lasting for hours in which we went over the fine detail, cross-checking our timeline of events built on a series of enormous spreadsheets.

The three of us agreed on the Ainsworths. We felt the evidence meant the case was more likely to be a double murder than a murder-suicide. Hurst, Davies, Chancellor and Grant Graham had all made the case that the lack of blood on Howard's clothes and hands simply didn't add up. The blood spatter evidence didn't make sense for a murder-suicide. Then there were the unexplained injuries to Howard's lips, the tell-tale signs of a hand clamped over his mouth; the lack of drugs in his system; the contradictory suicide letter; and the washing-down of the murder weapon in the sink.

But when it came to the Wards, there was disagreement, despite Steve Chancellor's view that it contained the most inconsistencies. Jonathan was concerned by the findings of Donald's blood on the light switch in the kitchen and on the outside of the knife drawer. He found it hard to believe the killer could have walked Donald downstairs to collect the knives, only to force him back upstairs to the bedroom to meet his death. George offered an alternative theory. What if Donald had escaped the bedroom and run downstairs to grab some weapons to then use against the attacker. Perhaps for a moment he considered escaping the house to raise the alarm, which would explain the keys in the door with the blood on them, but then, changing his mind, ran back upstairs to try to save Auriel.

I found Donald an unlikely killer. The act itself was completely incongruous with the man people knew. He was gentle, kind, compassionate – maybe a little pretentious, but always willing to put his family first. He was conscientious with his health and was visiting the doctor and having health checks in order to prolong his life. But he fretted about suspected ailments, and was far from brave when it came to his own well-being. The idea that Donald had the physical courage to cut his own throat and stab himself in the heart seemed to contradict everything we knew about his personality.

The doubts over his case did not simply rest on the report by Stephanie Davies. Her own conclusions had been built on the testimony of her predecessor, Christine Hurst, two investigators from the National Crime Faculty, Arthur Chancellor, a renowned FBI-trained investigator, and Grant Graham, a leading forensics expert. How could Donald have stabbed his own heart after cutting his jugular vein? How did he have a blood pattern stain on his face when he was found staring up at the ceiling? If Donald had pulled up the bedclothes, where were the bloody hand marks? The words of Nicholas Rheinberg, the

Cheshire coroner, kept returning to me: 'This in all respects was so alien to Mr Ward's personality – his whole life – that not a single shred of evidence would suggest there was a time bomb waiting to explode.'

There was one more task to be carried out before publication of the article. We wanted to ask Stephanie Davies herself if she wanted to comment. I knew from the beginning she would be unlikely to talk to us because she was employed by Cheshire Police, who would not want one of its senior employees discussing such matters with a journalist. Later, I became her friend, and supported her as the police turned against her. I would hear her side of the story in full.

But in August 2020, we were strangers. The source who had leaked the report to us had done so in the belief the police were not taking the concerns it raised seriously enough. That source was not Stephanie Davies. I knew she would be shocked to hear we had read it, but in the interests of fairness, she had to be warned we had the report before we published it. She had to be given the opportunity to discuss the report's findings.

On Friday afternoon, two days before we went to print, I parked my car outside her house on a new-build housing estate in Warrington. It was around 1 p.m. I wasn't sure if Davies would be working from home or at her office in Warrington Town Hall. I rang the doorbell of her little corner house and she opened the front door almost straight away. I knew it was her. She looked to be in her early thirties rather than early forties. Dark hair. Bright blue eyes. A computer screen was flickering in the background.

'Can I help?'

'I'm a reporter for the *Sunday Times*. We're running a story about your report into the Wilmslow murder suicides. We'd like to know if you could talk about it?'

She turned pale. At one point I wondered if she might faint. I braced myself to catch her. 'I can't say anything about that.'

She refused to comment, insisting that I speak to the Cheshire Police press office. It was a brief encounter, but at least she was informed of the situation.

The same day, we contacted Cheshire Police's communications team to provide them with advance notification of our story, and they provided the following statement for publication:

> We are in receipt of the report [Davies Review] and it is being reviewed. This is a piece of research which has been undertaken by the staff member, independently from her role within the constabulary. As with any case that has been closed, where new information comes to light, it is reviewed and acted upon if appropriate. We have notified both Greater Manchester Police and Cumbria Constabulary.

The statement failed to mention that Davies had actually first handed a draft of her report to the police in September 2018. She had waited for feedback which never came. On 23 August 2020, our Insight investigation into the Wilmslow killings was published on the front page of the *Sunday Times* headlined: BRUTAL DEATHS OF ELDERLY COUPLES SPARK FEAR OF SERIAL KILLER AT LARGE. The story was followed up by the BBC, ITV, Sky News, the *Independent*, *Daily Telegraph*, *Guardian*, *Daily Mail*, *Irish* and *Scottish Daily Mail*, *Sun*, *Daily Mirror*, *Manchester Evening News*, *Daily Star*, *Cheshire Chronicle*, London

Evening Standard, *Liverpool Echo*, *Macclesfield Express*, *Knutsford Guardian* and *Westmorland Gazette,* as well as news websites around the world. The next day the *Daily Mail* ran a special report from one of its senior journalists, Paul Bracchi, headlined: FEARS OVER SILVER KILLER: FIVE FRAIL COUPLES BRUTALLY SLAIN. FIVE APPARENT 'MURDER SUICIDES'. BUT NOW SECRET REPORT CLAIMS THERE COULD BE A PSYCHOPATH ON THE LOOSE. It was the first time the term 'silver killer' had been used.

That week, Cheshire Police set up a team to look into the findings of the Davies Review, led by the force's head of crime, who was to report to a chief officer. The police refused to reopen the cases for the time being, but did agree to conduct a paper review of the report to determine whether or not they should carry out a fresh inquiry. It had been almost two years since Davies first handed over her evidence. Finally, the police were taking an interest, but only after a series of reports about the murders in the *Sunday Times*. Members of the Ward family spoke to the press, supporting a new investigation into the case.

On 25 August 2020, the *Daily Mirror* ran a story headlined: SERIAL KILLER IS PLAUSIBLE . . . DON WAS A GENTLE CHAP. The article, by the news reporter Matthew Young, said that 'shocked relatives of a couple who suffered horrific deaths in 1999 have backed a probe into whether the pair were slain by a serial killer'. 'The police should certainly investigate this,' a relative of the Wards was quoted as saying. 'It's come as quite a shock. I have never been convinced about Donald killing anybody. He was a very gentle chap. Many relatives have now died thinking Donald killed Auriel. So if there is truth in this, it makes it even harder.'

The *Daily Mail* Northern Correspondent Liz Hull interviewed family members of Michael Higgins for an article headlined: HE HAD PARKINSON'S – HE WAS NO MURDERER. Michael's niece, Adele Street, and sister-in-law, Lily Higgins, said they had always doubted that Michael was capable of such a terrible crime. At the family home in Chorlton, Manchester, Adele said: 'They were 100 per cent murdered – without a doubt. He had severe Parkinson's disease – he was really shaky. He was not capable of doing such things. We have never, ever thought that he did it. He just did not have the strength. The new investigation is very welcome, but it is heartbreaking for the family to go through all this.'

She dismissed the idea that Michael had snapped because his wife had threatened to leave him and put him in a care home. 'That is rubbish,' she said. 'They were very decent, law-abiding people. There must be someone who had gained their confidence.' Adele's mother, married to Michael's younger brother, Daniel, added: 'He was not a violent man. We just want the truth to come out for the future generations of the family.'

The reactions of the families were mixed. Some believed the police had got it right the first time. Paul Sims, the *Sun's* Yorkshire Correspondent, wrote an article published on 24 August 2020 headlined SERIAL KILLER IN OUR MIDST?, quoting Kenneth and Eileen Martin's ex-son-in-law Dennis Tong, now sixty-three, who with his ex-wife Elaine had found their bodies. He remained convinced that it was a murder-suicide. 'Ken must have done it on the spur of the moment,' he said. 'I think he just crumbled under the pressure of looking after Eileen who had dementia.' Stanley Wilson's son, Graham, meanwhile, who lived in Kendal in Cumbria, was quoted in the same article saying, 'It was just a tragedy caused by my father's illness.'

The week after the *Sunday Times* article, Cheshire Police released a second, more expansive statement relating to the Davies Review. 'Cheshire Constabulary is aware of numerous news articles suggesting the possibility of a link between five historic murder-suicide cases comprising of two incidents in Cheshire, two in Greater Manchester and one in Cumbria,' the statement read.

> Detective Chief Superintendent Aaron Duggan said: 'These articles were based upon a report completed by a member of police staff working in the coroner's office in Cheshire. The report was not approved by either the constabulary or the coroner's office. Some media reports have referred to the author as a senior coroner or coroner and this is factually incorrect. The circumstances by which the report was shared with the media are subject to an internal review. The contents of the report and its conclusions are being considered by detectives. At this time, there is no reason to believe that the cases were not investigated by the police appropriately. They were also the subject of inquests. For these reasons, the constabulary has not re-opened the cases, however this decision will remain under review.'

To many, it appeared that the police were already attempting to distance themselves from the findings of their own senior coroner's officer. Stephanie Davies wanted justice for the families. She had written her report hoping that the police would re-open the cases and conduct a full forensic review of the evidence in storage relating to the Wilmslow killings. Three forces had agreed to conduct a paper review into the murder-suicides on their patches. That wasn't enough for her. It wouldn't be enough to catch the silver killer.

Stephanie Davies' own life was about to be turned upside down by a new criminal inquiry, one which would focus on her conduct while compiling the report for Cheshire Police's senior detectives; an inquiry which would put her career, reputation and livelihood at risk.

18

Reprisals

Stephanie Davies was sitting on her sofa feeling slightly nauseous as she waited for the doorbell to ring. It was the morning of 23 September 2020. Her solicitor, organised by her union, Unison, had warned her that Cheshire Police's dreaded standards department, the PSD, were going to arrive at her house at nine to serve her with misconduct papers. Her father had warned her to be careful. He had questioned why she had to be served with the papers at her home? Why could this not happen at police headquarters? Or in Warrington Town Hall? Davies was starting to wonder if he was right.

She had been on sick leave since being notified that the PSD, overseen by Detective Superintendent Warren, would be carrying out an investigation into how she had compiled her report into the Wilmslow killings. She was suspected of sharing confidential coroner's files with external experts without permission and leaking her report to the media.

She was still stunned by the development. Sharing information with experts outside Cheshire Police was all part of working for the coroner service. It was arguable that, although the work was conducted in her spare time, it was her job to investigate deaths in the county on behalf of the coroner. In the course of private research she had uncovered what she believed to be a killer who hadn't been caught. Sharing material from the coroner's files with trusted experts, all from law enforcement backgrounds, seemed entirely proportionate and in keeping with the public interest. In addition, she had been open with one of the chief inspectors about sharing her review with outside experts. She hadn't hidden anything. In fact, it was quite the opposite. She had submitted her review to senior officers – twice. The police's PSD investigation seemed excessive, and she hoped it was simply a box-ticking exercise, a way for the top brass to keep their noses clean while they got on with the real work of finding the murderer.

The first to arrive at her house was Detective Chief Inspector Chris Williams, her assigned welfare officer. She knew Williams had a high regard for her in a professional capacity and that he would have her back. Next to turn up was her union representative, followed by three female detectives from the PSD.

The PSD are the unit every copper and civilian staff member hope never to hear from. Most don't get so lucky. Somewhere along the line, everybody gets a complaint, often from a disgruntled criminal keen to get their own back, or sometimes from a victim unhappy with how their case was handled. Cheshire's PSD was responsible for ensuring the force maintained and enhanced its reputation and the service it provided to the public. Part of that service was the investigation of allegations made by the public about misconduct committed by either officers or police staff. They were the real AC-12 from *Line of Duty*.

The final person to arrive was a member of the police's IT support staff. He was told by the detectives to wait outside as there were too many people in the house to socially distance in order to stay safe from coronavirus infection. Davies was baffled. What could all these people possibly want? Why was a member of IT staff sitting in his car outside her house? *What on earth was happening?*

One of the PSD detectives stepped forward. She was pretty, in her thirties, wearing a dark suit jacket. She delivered the news in a polite and professional manner, as though reading a weather report. 'We've got a warrant to obtain all documents relating to the murder-suicide cases, your work laptop and work mobile, and your personal laptop and your personal mobile phone,' she said. 'I have a list of allegations against you which I have to read out, okay?'

Davies' eyes flicked to the thick bundle of paperwork in the detective's hands. On the top page she read the words 'criminal investigation' and 'gross misconduct'. Her stomach felt empty. A vein thudded at the side of her head. *Criminal investigation? Gross misconduct?*

Davies didn't know it yet, but two of the three detectives currently standing in her living room had been appointed by Detective Superintendent Warren to investigate a complaint about her from a member of the public in relation to leaking her report to the *Sunday Times*. Davies had not leaked her report. But the police had decided to investigate the claim at the same time as finding out how she had carried out her research. They wanted to know if her report had been work undertaken as part of her doctorate research, or a separate piece of research that had been self-generated. They wanted to establish the extent to which Cheshire Police and the coroner for Cheshire were aware of Davies' review of those cases, and what measures had been undertaken to ensure there were appropriate safeguards to mitigate any 'data protection issues'.

Part of their inquiry would look into how Davies had accessed policing information and whom she had shared her report with, both internally and externally. At the conclusion of their inquiry, there would be an assessment carried out as to whether there was a case to answer for misconduct or gross misconduct, which could mean dismissal. The PSD would also decide if the matter should be referred to the Crown Prosecution Service (CPS) for criminal charges under the Police (Conduct) Regulations 2020. Possible charges could be misconduct in a public office and various data protection breaches.

The detective read through the allegations. Davies was accused of carrying out detailed research into the deaths of Howard and Florence Ainsworth, and Donald and Auriel Ward. 'Both of these cases had been investigated by Cheshire Police and had been examined through the coronial process,' said the detective sternly. 'The outcome following inquest was recorded as murder-suicide. You prepared a report which set out your research into these deaths and a conclusion that the cases were in fact double murders and, as such, an offender could be outstanding.'

The officer said the material used to prepare the report was taken from the police's own investigations. The report was shared with a number of external experts when she had 'no permission to share policing information in this way'. 'It is alleged there was no policing purpose for sending the report containing police information to third-party individuals or sharing the information,' the detective said. Davies was aghast. *No purpose?*

She was told a member of the public had complained about a possible leak to the media. On the basis of researching the complaint, other allegations had been identified following an audit of the police systems, which would form the basis of the PSD inquiry. While the PSD inquiry was carried out, her duties as the senior coroner's officer would be restricted. She would no longer be in charge of her team — her deputy was going to take over. Her access to force systems would be restricted. She would be offered access to Cheshire Police's occupational health provider or the confidential care line if she felt the need to speak to somebody.

After the allegations were read out, the detectives started the house search. They wanted her laptop. Davies went upstairs to get it. The computer had her PhD research on it. She walked back downstairs with it. For a moment, her welfare officer, DCI Williams, thought Davies might crack it over the head of one of the PSD detectives. She breathed deeply and slammed it down on her desk instead.

'Phone?' said one of the detectives.

Davies was given a few seconds to scribble down some telephone numbers on a scrap of paper before her mobile phone was taken. The phone was specially adapted for a deaf person. It would leave her cut off from her friends and family. She felt as if her head was about to explode. She stepped through the back door into her garden and breathed the cold air. It was a sunny day, but she couldn't see colour. Everything was grey — the trees, the flowers, the grass. For a moment she considered running to the railway tracks near her house. She quickly pushed the thought from her mind. That wasn't her. She wasn't going to be beaten by this. She went back into the house.

'You okay, Steph?' Williams asked.

'Fine,' she responded, knowing that she wasn't.

The detectives had searched the house and gathered up paperwork, documents and electronic devices they felt were relevant to their misconduct investigation. They had taken her specially adapted personal and work Samsung mobile phones; a Microsoft tablet she used for work; a second tablet she kept for personal use; her HP laptop computer; a job application prep file; her personal 'dream diary'; two more personal diaries from 2016 and 2018; and some further documentation relating to her health. They seized a number of printed-off copies of her report, and a bundle of documents taken from news articles referencing murder-suicides across the UK. They also took documents relating to Steve Chancellor's own report into the Wilmslow cases.

But they weren't finished yet. The police IT technician entered the house carrying an electronic device and scanned each room for any hidden electronic devices which picked up a Wi-Fi signal. Computers. Tablets. Mobile phones. The detectives wanted to be certain they had everything.

After they were satisfied they hadn't missed anything, the young female detective turned to Davies. 'There will be an interview under caution,' she said. 'That will happen soon. You'll have to get a solicitor for it. Just to be clear, you've not been arrested.' They gave Davies a basic mobile phone as a temporary replacement for the handsets they had bagged up as evidence, but the phone didn't have the correct technology fitted for a deaf person. The PSD team left her house. Her hands shaking, Davies picked up her landline phone and called her father. She couldn't hear what he was saying, but she was able to speak to him. 'Dad. It's Steph. I can't hear you, but I need you to come to my house. Please, come quickly.'

She felt as though her life had just blown up. For the first time in her life, she knew how it felt to be the subject of a criminal investigation. She was the senior coroner's officer for Cheshire Police, a role which meant leading a team of thirteen people. She had personally investigated and processed more than 5,000 deaths in the county of Cheshire. She had won commendations for her work. The coronavirus pandemic had made her job even more demanding, but she had risen to that challenge, working excess hours, weekends and bank holidays to cope with the demand. She had helped with strategic planning as part of Cheshire's excess deaths forum along with Cheshire Police, the local authorities, NHS England, North West Ambulance Service, Clinical Commissioning Groups, and funeral directors and mortuaries. She had provided advice to doctors and front-line police officers which had prevented mortuaries reaching maximum capacity, while arranging the right equipment for her team members to work from home during lockdown.

Her team had been nominated for an award as a result of her leadership during the pandemic, which ensured Cheshire's mortuaries were not overwhelmed. Davies had never had so much as a speeding ticket, and now she was being treated like a criminal for acting on the suspicions of her predecessor, regarded as one of the most experienced coroner's officers in the history of the service. She was being punished for seeking outside advice for her report, despite coroner's officers sharing sensitive information every day with pathologists, mortuary staff, toxicologists, doctors, hospitals, independent medical staff and family members. Indeed, the job would be practically impossible without it.

Davies had wanted justice for the families. But instead of helping the detectives in their hunt for a killer, she now found herself the subject of a major criminal investigation, which threatened to leave her career in tatters.

When Cheshire Police transferred to its £40 million purpose-built headquarters in Winsford, people would often remark about the building's passing resemblance to the Pentagon, home of the US Department of Defense. It was a far cry from the constabulary's first home at No. 4 Seller Street in Chester, a two-bed terrace house close to the Shropshire Union Canal Main Line which used to double up as the home of the chief constable. More than 1,000 officers and staff from 45 different departments now work in Winsford, which feels more like the headquarters of a major global corporation than a police station.

On 8 October 2020, Davies attended force headquarters for a voluntary interview under caution. Accompanied by her solicitor, she was ushered into a conference room by two PSD detectives: the young female detective who had been part of the house search and a second female detective, this one older, in her fifties, with blonde hair and hard eyes. Davies recognised the conference room: she had used it a few months ago to deliver a three-hour talk to the new class of detectives about investigating sudden deaths. Her lecture to around thirty officers had covered topics such as staged crime scenes and how to spot them, 999 call analysis, and ways of identifying guilty offenders through their phone calls from crime scenes. She had been singled out for praise by Emma Myers, one of Cheshire's crime trainers. 'A morbid but absolutely fascinating talk from a very knowledgeable speaker,' Myers said in her written feedback. 'I think my favourite of all the presentations. A lot of knowledge to absorb which should guide thinking in future.'

The detectives told her a hearing loop had been installed in the room, a special sound system which produces a wireless signal picked up by hearing aids. Davies told the officers it was not necessary. She asked them to remove their coronavirus masks so she could lip-read as they asked questions. Davies confirmed her full name and date of birth. She was then cautioned.

'Stephanie Davies, you do not have to say anything. But it may harm your defence if you do not mention when questioned something which you later rely on in court,' said the younger female detective. 'Anything you do say may be given in evidence.' The offences being investigated were Misconduct in a Public Office contrary to Common Law, and Section 170 of the Data Protection Act 2018.

Davies' solicitor handed over a twenty-three-page defence statement. The statement laid out her entire case and explained exactly how she had gone about compiling her report. Davies believed it was within her role and responsibility as senior coroner's officer to review the Wilmslow cases and take appropriate action where needed. She wanted to present a compelling report to the police and coroner to initiate an inquiry. She had access to the coroner's files both in the coroner's office and the coroner's archive at the town hall. To get those files she would either ask one of the coroner's administrative team to retrieve an archived file or she would retrieve it herself.

After reviewing the relevant documents relating to the

Wilmslow cases, she believed writing a report was the best way to record her observations and highlight her concerns with senior police officers. She consulted with experts from different fields in order to make her report more compelling and have her concerns taken seriously. She took advice from experts in bloodstain pattern analysis, wound pattern analysis, staged crime scene investigation, criminal profiling, crime scene analysis, suicide note authentication and cold case investigation.

She claimed that a senior police officer had been aware that she had approached external experts for the purposes of her report. She was only told to stop working on the review when the police force became aware that it may have been leaked to the *Sunday Times*. She believed her report served the public interest and the sharing of material with relevant experts was carried out in good faith in what was simply an extension of her role as a sudden-death investigator for the police. Much of the material she had shared with those experts was already in the public domain since the cases had been heard in full public inquests. She believed it was her moral and ethical duty to bring the conclusions of her review to the attention of the police and ultimately the coroner.

Jonathan, George and I talked about the possible consequences for Davies in the run-up to publishing details of her report in the *Sunday Times*. She had not provided us with her report and had given us no information or help before we published. Although we accepted there would no doubt be some serious questions raised by her superiors about how her report had reached the public domain, her defence would simply be the truth: 'It was not me.' The informant was concerned that the file was being kept in a locked drawer at police headquarters, destined never to see the light of day. As far as we were concerned, Davies was simply doing her job. She had raised a matter of significant public interest in her report: she believed a killer may have been missed by the police, and after many months of investigation, so did we. We knew that a story in the *Sunday Times* might give the police more motivation to investigate the killings. But in the end, Cheshire Police's investigations into Davies lasted longer than their inquiries into the murders themselves.

Davies gave the detectives her defence statement and the police interview was terminated while they went away to read it. She was called back to headquarters two weeks later for a second interview. This time the interview was in a small classroom with a projector screen and desks. Davies and her solicitor sat at desks positioned side by side. The two female PSD detectives were sitting opposite them with a recording device. They bombarded Davies with more than 200 questions in the space of three hours. On the advice of her solicitor she answered 'No comment.' She had already explained everything they needed to know in her defence statement. She wasn't hiding anything.

'When did you submit the first report?'

No comment.

'You were careless. You lost control of that data, didn't you?'

No comment.

'Or did you know what you were doing?'

No comment.

'Did you share that report deliberately so it would leak to the press?'

No comment.

One of the PSD detectives read out entries from Davies' personal diaries. Davies had written about a passing crush on a detective chief inspector. Now PSD was trying to use her private diaries against her.

'You had a crush on that senior officer, didn't you?'

No comment.

'You leaked your report to the press on purpose because he rejected you, didn't you?'

No comment.

'We've read your diaries. You were incapable of making any rational decisions at the time which would have affected the findings of your report, wouldn't it?'

No comment.

After the interviews, Davies was left in a state of limbo. She was officially 'off sick', still being paid by the force, but no longer working for the coroner service. PSD carried on with their investigations into Davies, while separately, Cheshire, Greater Manchester and Cumbria police forces examined the findings of the Davies Review. On 15 January 2021, Detective Superintendent Chris Warren, from Cheshire Police's Professional Standards Department, sent her a letter officially suspending her from her duties. Two months later, Warren sent Davies another letter, informing her that a file of evidence had been sent to the Crown Prosecution Service (CPS) for consideration.

Nobody likes to be told they are wrong or have made a mistake during the course of their work. That is part of human nature. Police officers are no different in this respect. Except the consequences can be far greater. Mistakes in investigations can lead to miscarriages of justice. The wrong person could be charged and sentenced for a crime they have not committed, while the real offender remains at large. In the cases of the Ainsworths and the Wards, there is evidence which contradicts the conclusion that Howard Ainsworth and Donald Ward were responsible. However, there is also evidence which contradicts the idea that a third party was responsible. Either way, there is no neat answer to explain what happened in Wilmslow in 1996 and 1999. Only by returning to the very start, placing each case side by side, and using the latest forensic techniques to pick apart what remains of the evidence kept in storage, is there a chance of being certain of the truth – something which, so far, Cheshire Police has refused to do.

Rooted in this story is an obvious concern about a killer who may have been missed. This book has discussed how detective work and the tools available to detectives have changed remarkably since the '90s, when the Wilmslow killings took place, partly owing to the leaps made in the rapidly evolving world of forensic science, but also because of reforms carried out to modernise police work in response to bungled investigations. Perhaps it is time for the police to adapt and evolve once again, or risk being left behind by a new breed of killer. Offenders are changing their behaviour. The 'CSI effect' means even the average member of the public has awareness of the forensic techniques used by the police to catch criminals. TV and Netflix are full of documentaries which go into painstaking detail about how detectives snared their suspect. Offenders are more likely than ever to take precautions before a crime, clean up afterwards and mislead investigators by altering a crime scene. Crimes committed on impulse can leave behind more evidence linking the offender to the scene. But killers who plan their crimes beforehand will carry them out when there are no witnesses. They might use gloves. Even leave a note purporting to be the victim's last words.

The police inquiry into the deaths of the Ainsworths quickly determined that Howard murdered his wife. This had a ripple effect. The police did not consider the deaths of the Wards to be a comparable case when it was initially being treated as a murder inquiry. Two cases, side by side, which could have been the work of a single offender. At the time of the Wilmslow killings, detectives had no formal training in how to spot a staged crime scene. It was something passed down informally, detective to detective, sergeant to constable. A skill learnt 'on the job'. Twenty years later, there is still no formal training in spotting staged crime scenes. In this respect, US law enforcement agencies, led by the FBI, are leagues ahead.

The coroner's service, which could act as a backstop in flagging such cases, also has weaknesses. Loopholes in the coroner system were once ruthlessly exploited by the serial killer Dr Harold Shipman. Shipman, a general practitioner in Greater Manchester, would falsify the details on death certificates, murdering up to 250 patients between 1971 and 1998. As a family GP, Shipman was in a position to certify the cause of death and in many cases persuaded relatives of the victims there was no need for a post-mortem examination, which might have revealed the diamorphine drugs he had injected into his patients while killing them. Shipman's methods exposed the cracks in the system between the police and the coroner. About 80 per cent of his victims were elderly women, though it was suspected by police he had killed patients as young as four. After his conviction, changes to the system of how death certificates are issues were recommended by a public inquiry in 2005, which Christine Hurst gave evidence to. But the judge who led the Shipman inquiry, Dame Janet Smith, would later criticise the government for putting 'hardly any' of her recommendations into place. She believed that the reason the coroner service was not properly reformed was a general perception in government that Shipman was a 'one-off'.

Improvements to the coroner service were made by the Coroners and Justice Act 2009, implemented in 2013, which created a chief coroner. Guidance and training improved. But concerns remain about the variation in standards across different areas. Christine Hurst and Stephanie Davies saw first-hand the flaws in the system. In cases where the death is deemed suspicious it is the police, not the coroner's officers, who will investigate to establish the facts for the coroner. But in their view, coroners could be too easily swayed by the findings of the police. This system is further weakened by coroner's officers becoming increasingly office-bound. Many of them lack the necessary skills or training to flag inconsistencies. Hurst and Davies questioned the findings of the police, but were forced to take an informal route to do so. Hurst had several meetings with police officers. Her concerns were largely ignored. Davies submitted a report, which was eventually examined, but only after the *Sunday Times* wrote a series of articles about its findings, forcing the hand of Cheshire Police. A bolstered service of coroner's officers, with the skills and training to identify inconsistencies in equivocal deaths and a formal route to making recommendations to the coroner, together with the power to force detectives to take another look, could help prevent mistakes made at the crime scene going any further. They could act as a safety net, a second pair of eyes. It could help remove doubt from the system.

Stephanie Davies took it upon herself to do what she thought was right. She investigated the Wilmslow killings and wrote a report which concluded they were not murder-suicides, but double murders. Her report was supported by experts in their field. But the police refused to act upon its warnings, and instead chose to spend money and resources to investigate their own senior coroner's officer for doing what she thought was best for the families of the victims. She was punished for doing what should be her job.

Stephen Lawrence was once the victim of a racist murder. The aftermath of the incompetent inquiry to catch his murderers created a turning point for the police. It forced detectives to modernise and equip themselves with the tools necessary to drag criminal investigations out of the Victorian era and into the twenty-first century. But the police face a new challenge, and they must evolve once more to catch a new type of killer. It is a killer more subtle than anything we have seen before: an unfortunate by-product, perhaps, of our own fascination with murder. A killer who might be able to sneak into the homes of two elderly couples in the same sleepy Cheshire town to carry out the most appalling murders and get away with it. Because there is one fact that must be true. If you decide that Donald Ward could not have killed himself by slitting his own throat and stabbing himself in the heart, then whatever remains, no matter how improbable, must be the truth.

EPILOGUE

Cracks in the System

The leaves whipped around my shoes as I walked down an eerily quiet street of nondescript houses. A dog barked in the distance, somewhere out of sight. I was heading towards one house in particular, which I could see just at the bottom of the road.

I had spent months working with the *Sunday Times* Insight team investigating the evidence. We had tried exhaustively to track down families, friends, work colleagues, neighbours and police officers connected to the Wilmslow murder-suicide cases. Over the course of that research we had heard theories about a number of potential suspects. We even received a number of tips, some anonymous, about who the killer might be. One such tip was from a concerned Wilmslow resident who suspected a person involved in the medical profession who might have known intimate details of each of the couples' circumstances and been able to take advantage of them at their most vulnerable. Or could it be a rogue member of a euthanasia society? Or a con artist who had befriended the couples and was able to enter their homes without being perceived as a threat?

Each of the names given to us had their own strengths and weaknesses. But there was one suspect in particular who caught our attention. His name is known to many detectives within Cheshire Police. He was not an easy person to find. Searching for him in the system was like looking for a ghost. But after several months, I finally located where he was living.

I walked down his street, wondering what I would find at the end of my story: a monster who carried out sadistic attacks for his own pleasure on some of the most vulnerable people in society, or a completely innocent man? Whatever I was about to discover, for legal reasons I could never report it. Accusing an individual of being a serial killer would require an extraordinary level of evidence which, unfortunately, I do not have.

Cheshire Police has refused to reopen the Wilmslow cases and its paper review of the original findings is over. As such, it is unlikely the silver killer suspect will ever be investigated in a meaningful way. Cold cases are notoriously difficult to crack, and the crimes some believe he committed are more than two decades old. The advances of forensic science offer a glimmer of hope. Very little else can help solve a murder investigation after such a long period of time, unless, of course, somebody out there knows something. If so, I can only hope they can summon the courage to speak to the police.

For me, it was the end of the road for this story, one of the greatest mysteries I have encountered, which grew out of the canteen gossip of Macclesfield Police Station and those coroner's files which sat in the Special Interest box, forgotten for decades. Christine Hurst and Stephanie Davies believe there is a killer out there. So does Steve Chancellor. The tabloids call him the silver killer, because he targets elderly people in their homes. The suspect for those murders is still at large in the community. I arrived at his doorstep and knocked on his door.

The rest, I can never talk about.

In February 2021, after seven months investigating what became known as the Davies Review, Cheshire Police released a third statement on the Wilmslow killings.

> *In August 2020, Cheshire Constabulary became aware of a report that called into question the findings of detectives in relation to a number of historic homicide cases in Cheshire, Manchester and Cumbria. This was a piece of research which had been undertaken by a member of staff, independently from her role within the Constabulary. The contents of this document have been meticulously investigated by experienced detectives, who have established that the research contained no information that would undermine the original findings of the officers at the time. This has been validated by forensic science services and the National Crime Agency, and we are satisfied that there is no evidence to support further investigation into these matters. A similar review process has taken place in Manchester and Cumbria, both of which have reached the same conclusion. We have maintained a close contact with the families involved during this process, and hope they are reassured by the review's findings. Our thoughts remain with them.*

On 2 November 2021, more than a year after her house was raided, Cheshire Police wrote to Davies informing her that the Crown Prosecution Service (CPS) had decided no further action should be taken against her. Davies has vowed to continue her fight to uncover the truth about the Wilmslow murders.